A Culinary Exploration
of the World's Most
Versatile Ingredient

Egg

Michael Ruhlman

Photography by
Donna Turner Ruhlman

LITTLE, BROWN AND COMPANY
New York Boston London

Little, Brown and Company
Hachette Book Group
237 Park Avenue, New York, NY 10017
littlebrown.com

First Edition: April 2014

Little, Brown and Company is a division of Hachette Book Group, Inc.
The Little, Brown name and logo are trademarks of Hachette Book Group, Inc.

The publisher is not responsible for websites (or their content) that are not owned by the publisher.

The Hachette Speakers Bureau provides a wide range of authors for speaking events. To find out more, go to hachettespeakersbureau.com or call (866) 376-6591.

ISBN 978-0-316-25406-9
Library of Congress Control Number 2013948058

10 9 8 7 6 5 4 3 2

sc

Book and jacket design by Gary Tooth/Empire Design Studio

Printed in China

For Blake Bailey

Contents

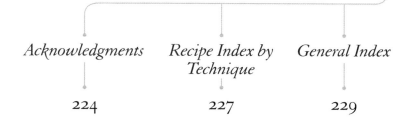

Why I Wrote a Book about the World's Most Versatile Ingredient

I was on the phone with author and television personality Alton Brown not long ago, whom I first met while taping season one of *The Next Iron Chef America*. He asked what I was working on.

"I want to write about the egg," I said, "all the things you can do with an egg, and how if you knew everything about cooking with eggs, you would become a better cook in a hundred different ways."

He said, "Yeah, I've always liked to say that the egg is the Rosetta stone of the kitchen."

That is exactly what makes Alton Brown so good on TV—he cuts right to the chase with the perfect metaphor: an ancient stone that helped us decipher a little-known language. Like that Rosetta stone, the egg, far more ancient, unlocks the secret language of the kitchen. Learn the language of the egg—understand completely this amazing and beautiful oblong orb—and you can enter new realms of cooking, rocketing you to stellar heights of culinary achievement.

The greatest of all our foods, the egg combines beauty, elegance, and simplicity, a miracle of natural design and, as food, bounty. Containing all of the nutrients required to create life, eggs give our bodies a powerful combination of proteins, amino acids, fatty acids, antioxidants, minerals, and vitamins, a package unmatched by any other single food.

The egg represents food at an almost primordial level when we eat it raw, consuming the liquidy stuff of life itself, and is capable of being transformed into the most sophisticated of culinary creations. I think of my friend and collaborator Thomas Keller and his truffle custard—egg and cream flavored with white truffle, cooked and served in the shell with a potato chip garnish. It's one of the finest four-star dishes ever created, and it's nothing more than egg, cream, truffle, potato. Genius in its simplicity.

The egg's shell is delicate but sturdy, porous but protective. Inside, more than a dozen different proteins form the white, the albumen, each serving a specific function in the developing creature—some feeding the embryo, some fending off large predators, others disabling harmful microbes. It's evolution at its most elegant and offers the cook a range of culinary acrobatics that give us an airy cake, a crisp meringue, a pillowy soufflé, or a tightly bound seafood terrine.

The yolk, that rich and fatty orb—suspended at either end within the albumen by protein coils called chalazae—is the nutrient center of the egg, accounting for three-quarters of the egg's calories. It also contains iron, thiamin, vitamin A, protein, cholesterol, and lecithin (a badass fat-water-hybrid molecule that gives yolks the ability to emulsify a lot of fat into a small amount of water, for culinary essentials such as the humble mayonnaise and the elegant béarnaise sauce).

A miracle of nature ought to be rare, like a truffle, but the egg is abundant; it ought likewise to be expensive, but instead it is among the most affordable foods in the store, costing just pennies apiece for the mass-produced varieties. At their very finest—from free-range hens fed only organic grain—eggs still cost only thirty or forty cents each.

The egg, as an individual food item (say, a poached egg on whole-wheat toast), is excellent. As an ingredient the egg is also, to the chef, an emblem and test of a cook's skill. More than with any other ingredient, the way an egg is handled by a cook tells a chef 90 percent of what he or she needs to know about a prospective hire. Many chefs ask a young cook to put aside the résumé and make an omelet. That's all that's needed as a tryout, because cooking an omelet well requires skill, knowledge, experience, and finesse.

It's this fact that long ago started me thinking about the importance of the egg to cooking generally. I got down to the business of writing about the egg in *Ruhlman's Twenty*, devoting an entire chapter to it, beginning thus:

> If you could choose to master a single ingredient, no choice would teach you more about cooking than an egg. It is an end in itself; it's a multipurpose ingredient; it's an all-purpose garnish; it's an invaluable tool. The egg teaches your hands finesse and delicacy. It helps your arms develop strength and stamina. It instructs in the way proteins behave in heat and in the powerful ways we can change food mechanically. It's a lever for getting food to behave in great ways. Learn to take the egg to its many differing ends, and you've enlarged your culinary repertoire by a factor of ten.

For this book I wanted to write about all those differing ends, working my way back to the egg. And in thinking about those ends, I began to break down the egg into its many uses. It quickly developed in my head not as ends, or single recipes, but as a unity, a single complex image in which everything is connected. Nature loves simplicity and unity: the hen's egg is an expression of nature's genius.

In the kitchen, the egg is ultimately neither ingredient nor finished dish but rather a singularity with a thousand ends. Scrambled eggs and angel food cake and ice cream and aioli and popovers and *gougères* and *macarons* and a gin fizz aren't separate entities, they're all part of the egg continuum, they are all one thing. The egg is a lens through which to view the entire craft of cooking. By working our way through the egg, we become powerful cooks.

Anyone familiar with my work knows my belief in the sanctity of technique. Recipes today are free. The world is awash in recipes. While there's nothing wrong with recipes per se, there's everything wrong with relying solely on recipes if you want to be a better cook. You've got to be very shrewd to disinter an unknown technique from within a recipe. But if you know a single technique, you immediately have hundreds of recipes at hand. That's why cooking schools don't teach recipes, they teach technique.

Recipes are a valuable resource for ideas, and I use them often. Sometimes they offer outright an unfamiliar technique. I love to compare recipes for the same finished product—*Why does this quick bread use both baking powder and baking soda? Why does that one use considerably more egg relative to the flour? What are the resulting differences?* When I'm writing my own recipes, I often compare various recipes, pick and choose elements from each that I like, filter them through my own particular nature (preferences, biases, practicalities, competencies), to arrive at a recipe that is more or less mine (I don't know that there are any truly unique recipes in traditional cooking). There are many wonderful recipes in this book, so even if you just want to get dinner on the table and have no desire to become a better cook, the preparations in this book will still make you feel like a star. The recipes have also been chosen because they are classic or distinctive examples of a technique made possible by the miraculous egg.

Within the universe of the egg are dozens of techniques. I'd wager that no other single ingredient has as many, not by a long shot. But shouldn't we expect as much from a little package that contains all the stuff of life itself?

THE EGG FLOWCHART

THE IDEA TO PRESENT THE EGG AS A FLOWCHART CAME NATURALLY, FROM JUST THINKing about it, asking the question, "What can you do with an egg?"

The answer—after the obvious "all kinds of things"—is that it depends. Are you going to cook it in its shell or out? If you're going to leave it in its shell, are you going to cook it hard or soft? If you're going to cook it out of its shell, are you going to cook it whole or separate it? Are you going to cook it at all? Are you going to use it as a tool, to leaven a cake or emulsify a mayonnaise?

You could even make a game of it. Think of a dish that uses eggs—a quiche, a cake, a poached egg, pasta carbonara—and your opponent has twenty guesses. You'd begin with those same questions—Is it cooked in the shell or out? If out, is it whole or separated? If separated, is the white or the yolk used? If used whole, is it cooked as is or blended?

It occurred to me that to show, visually, how versatile the egg is, I'd have to make a flowchart. After thinking about how readily egg preparations would lend themselves to a graphic representation in this format, I sat down at our dining room table with a roll of parchment paper and wrote one out. It was sloppy, the kind of diagram a teacher at a blackboard would improvise. But it worked—the egg really did present itself visually as a flowchart, one that measured about a foot and a half long.

When I was ready to get serious about it, I asked my wife and partner, Donna, to write it out, since she's better at all things visual. I mapped the whole thing out, and she figured out how much space she was going to need to get it all in. The finished diagram required a five-foot length of parchment.

It was a thing of beauty. It mesmerized. I tacked it across a row of bookshelves behind my desk, and when we had a gang over for a New Year's Day brunch, people went into my office and gazed as if it were a museum piece. By twos and threes, guests stood staring at it, pointing things out to each other, and staring some more. A few stood for ten minutes before they could draw themselves away. "Michael," they asked, "what *is* this?"

The promise of the flowchart demanded to be fulfilled. A removable poster of the flowchart is included at the back of this book.

THE WAY I COOK

MY DEAR EDITOR, MICHAEL SAND, SOMETIMES MAKES ME WANT TO PULL MY HAIR OUT. When I went page by page through his edit of the manuscript that would become this book, I saw that he was a comma freak. I kind of toss them willy-nilly onto the page after I've written it and hope they fall into the right places, and so am incredibly grateful for his fastidiousness. He is acutely attuned to confusing or lazy phrasings in a recipe and calls attention to them without making me feel like an idiot. His questions arrive with a delicacy that would please the famously decorous former *New Yorker* editor William Shawn.

But he continually asked me about butter (salted or unsalted?) and kept writing "large eggs?" in a book *about* eggs. Why do these most basic questions make me want to pull my hair out? Because *it doesn't matter.*

And because at the same time it *does* matter. (I could put three commas in that fragment but refuse to.)

And, finally, because it lasers in on the fundamental difficulty of writing about food: Cooking is so infinitely nuanced that to write completely about how to cook any dish would require a manuscript longer than a David Foster Wallace novel and include twice as many footnotes within twice as many endnotes. And then no one would be able to follow it, let alone cook from it—and just as well, because it would *still* be incomplete. That's how nuanced cooking is.

I'm not a chef but I am a cook; I've written with, and for, a lot of really talented chefs, and there isn't a single one I haven't learned something from—and then incorporated it into my own way of cooking or adapted it to my culinary personality, which is not fussy or detail-oriented, but rather exuberant and life-embracing.

Salt is the most valuable ingredient in the kitchen. Thomas Keller told me this sixteen years ago, when I asked him what he considered the most important thing for a cook to know. After thinking for a little bit he said, "How to salt food. It's the first thing we teach new cooks when they come to work at the French Laundry."

Michael Symon taught me to salt onions the moment they hit the pan (I used to wait till I got at least *some* liquid in there). He does it to get the seasoning process under way, but when I did it I realized it also pulls out water and gets them cooking faster. That's how my personality fits into what he taught me. And Michael Symon didn't come up with this idea, he got it from another chef early in his own career. Michael Pardus taught me how to salt pasta water ("till it *tastes* seasoned"), Eric Ripert taught me how to salt fish, Judy Rodgers taught me how to salt meat, and again Keller, who has taught me so much I don't know where he ends and I begin, taught me that it didn't matter what kind of salt I used, but rather that the critical factor was using the *same* salt every time so that my fingers got used to a specific quantity.

Probably the most important thing I taught myself, when I wanted to convert an older chef's ratios into contemporary ones for a book, was how important weighing your food is as opposed to measuring it by volume. It makes all of cooking so much easier and more consistent. So, if you have a scale, use it, especially for measuring flour and large quantities of salt.

See? I could go on and on about just salt and we haven't even gotten to how to use it in a recipe or how it affects butter (it's added for flavor), and it doesn't have anything to do with eggs (except that it makes them taste better). So Michael Sand's question about salted or un-salted butter requires an essay, but I'll try to boil it down to this: I use salted butter because it's what I've been using since I started cooking in the fourth grade; it's what I'm used to. And since even sweet preparations benefit from salt, salted butter works fine even in pastries. Most chefs use unsalted butter; this is because they want ultimate control over the salt level in their food. I have no issue with this. Indeed, salt levels are especially important in the pastry kitchen. On occasion it will be the butter I choose to use for this reason.

So what do we make of the fact that salted and unsalted butter yield pretty much the same results? We are to take from this a very important lesson: good cooking requires us to pay attention, to think, and to taste our food and evaluate it throughout the cooking process.

Which brings me to the "large egg" question. Large eggs, by definition in the United States, weigh 2 ounces. In his book *On Food and Cooking*, Harold McGee notes that large eggs weigh 55 grams (about 1 gram less than 2 ounces), with the whites weighing 38 grams and the yolks 17 grams. But the thing is, they don't all weigh exactly that—some "large" eggs weigh a little more, some a little less. Other sources will tell you that they weigh 50 grams and contain 70 calories, whereas McGee says they contain exactly 84 calories. Here's the truth: if you were to crack ten large eggs into a bowl, you'd find that they'd come pretty darn close to 550 grams total, 380 grams of white and 170 grams of yolk. (And if you have to worry about the calorie issue, you need to start eating smarter.)

Moreover, what if you're lucky enough to have a neighbor who raises hens and supplies you with really fresh eggs? They're going to be all different sizes, unless your neighbor has a government inspector living in the backyard to do the sorting. Either weigh them or just use your common sense.

If you want to be completely accurate, you do need to weigh your eggs, and many professional kitchens and bakeries do this. But for most preparations, this is neither practical nor necessary. So the rule is the same for salt, butter, and eggs, those most fundamental ingredients: it doesn't matter what kind you buy, what matters is that you always buy the same kind.

And pay attention.

For health and safety issues, see page 211.

ABOUT THE RECIPES IN THIS BOOK

LIKE ALL RECIPES, MINE ARE APPROXIMATIONS ONLY, AND SO REQUIRE THAT YOU PAY attention and adjust as you go. Food will behave differently in an arid Phoenix kitchen than it will in a humid North Carolina kitchen than it will in a mile-in-the-sky Denver kitchen. These recipes have all been tested, and they should work perfectly well no matter your location or equipment, especially since most are very simple anyway and allow for plenty of give.

As for the specifics, unless otherwise stated:

* All eggs are large.

* All flour is all-purpose unbleached.

* All salt is coarse kosher salt.

* All butter is salted; if you prefer unsalted butter, just
  pay attention to the flavor of the recipe you're cooking.

For successful and satisfying cooking, you don't need *lots* of equipment, but you do need *good* equipment. You need two good stainless-steel sauté pans (a big one and a little one), one big pot, and one medium saucepan. Occasionally a nonstick pan is useful, but usually it's not. You need a wooden spoon with a flat edge. You need a large, heavy cutting board. Many people hamper themselves by trying to cut up their food on a board the size of a sheet of paper. Give yourself plenty of room.

NUTRITIONAL DIFFERENCES IN EGGS

There will always be squabbling over food issues, so before you latch on to that 2010 *Time* magazine article that says that organic eggs are no more healthy for you than factory-farmed eggs, or side with the opposite camp (many organic proponents denounced the article), know what the labels mean (see box on next page), and use your common sense. While there's no definitive way to be sure of the nutritional content of every egg available to you, an independent study by researchers at Pennsylvania State University, published in the journal *Renewable Agriculture and Food Systems*, found that pastured hens produce more nutritious eggs than factory-farmed eggs. This makes good sense to me.

I will forever urge people to use their common sense first. In an ideal scenario you know the person who sells you the eggs and can ask about how the hens are raised and what they are fed. The Penn State study reported that pastured eggs have three times as much omega-3 fatty acids, twice as much vitamin E, and 40 percent more vitamin A in their yolks than factory-farmed eggs.

Some sources point out that eggs from pastured hens are also free of antibiotic residues and contain no arsenic, which is sometimes added to the feed of factory-farmed chickens to prevent infections and spur growth. Others claim there's no difference.

Given that what goes into our animals affects what comes out, it stands to reason that chickens feeding in a well-tended pasture, or enclosed chickens fed a diet of organic grain, will produce healthy, nutritious eggs. So, if you don't know the source of your eggs, pay attention to what the labels mean but don't worry too much either way, as long as you eat a healthy diet yourself. Even the cheapest of eggs are still nutritious and delicious.

A great alternative to buying eggs is to raise your own chickens, as many people are doing now. The trend is so strong that Williams-Sonoma advertises backyard chicken coops in its catalogs. This is a good option if you like this kind of work. I have one friend who has an egg intolerance; eating them makes her very uncomfortable. But she loves eggs, so she began raising a variety of hen breeds and found that one, Barred Rocks, produces eggs that don't make her ill.

Here are some online resources if you want to look into raising your own layers:

backyardchickens.com
beginningfarmers.org
hobbyfarms.com
mypetchicken.com

By far the biggest problem in home kitchens is the lack of a sharp knife. You need two of them, a big one and a little one. And they need to be sharp. A big knife block with forty-five knives of different sizes is useless if not one is sharp. Please, find a good knife sharpener in your area (preferably a wet-grind service, and not a hardware store that also does lawn mower blades) or buy a good sharpening stone (I swear by the DMT Diamond Whetstone sharpener). And learn how to use a sharpening steel to keep the edge.

After that it's all a matter of practice. And as far as I'm concerned, there's no better practice than that which results in a tasty, healthy meal for your family and your friends.

EGGS OF A DIFFERENT FEATHER

THIS BOOK IS DEVOTED SOLEly to chicken eggs, produced, packaged, and sold by the billions, a staple of kitchens worldwide, because laying chickens are the easiest and least expensive birds to raise

WHAT THE EGG LABELS MEAN

While you'll find a wide range of labels on egg cartons, the term "organic" seems to be the primary designation monitored and certified by the United States Department of Agriculture (USDA). Other labels placed on eggs and the way the hens are raised are not regulated by the USDA, although all commercial eggs have stamps noting when they were laid. Here are the definitions of other designations you may find in your grocery store's egg section.

CAGE-FREE

Hens that are allowed to roost and socialize freely in a room or an open area can be called cage-free; this open area is typically in a barn or poultry house. Cage-free chicken farming is more labor intensive and land intensive for the farmer, which is why these eggs tend to cost more. Being cage-free is regulated, but the USDA's definition is vague, giving more of an indication how the chicken was *not* raised (that is, confined to a cage).

FREE-RANGE

Eggs that are laid by hens that have access to the outdoors can be called free-range eggs. These hens have the same benefits as cage-free hens. However, "outdoors" designates only no roof, not necessarily the healthfulness of the environment in which they're raised—it could be on grass, dirt, or a few square feet of concrete.

PASTURE-RAISED

This is another unregulated term, but it does imply that the hens spend time outside on grass and eat a diet partly, if not entirely, of bugs and plants. This is the type of egg you're likely to find at a farmers' market.

ORGANIC

The USDA classifies and certifies eggs as organic, but the regulations can differ by state. Organic eggs are raised according to USDA National Organic Program guidelines and are marketed as such on the carton. These hens are allowed free range of their houses, given outdoor access (though time outside is not regulated), and fed an organic diet (meaning that the feed is not treated with pesticides, antibiotics, herbicides, or fertilizers). If the hens do not have access to pasture area, then the growers must provide the chickens with sprouted grains or fresh plants on a daily basis. Organic-egg producers put a USDA emblem on the carton denoting that the eggs are certified organic.

OMEGA-3 EGGS

These eggs come from hens that were fed a diet of foods rich in omega-3 fatty acids, such as algae, fish oil, and flaxseeds. By adjusting the hen's diet, the level of the omega-3s in the egg increases from 30 milligrams per egg to 100 to 600 milligrams per egg, according to some sources. The USDA does not certify this, but farms can be audited if they make such claims.

VEGETARIAN

This label denotes that no animal products have been used in the feed given to the hens.

NATURAL EGGS

This label does not indicate anything about how the chicken was raised; it simply means that no flavoring, brine, or color was added to the egg. The USDA does not regulate this designation.

NO HORMONES/ NO ANTIBIOTICS

These terms indicate that the grower has not used any hormones (prohibited by law) or antibiotics on the chicken itself or included them in its feed. The USDA does not certify this, but farms making such claims can be audited and must be able to document their claims.

AMERICAN HUMANE CERTIFIED

This label designates that the American Humane Association has deemed that the farm where the hens lay is humane according to its standards. The hens are raised in cage-free barns or warehouses; they are allowed to roost and socialize freely indoors; no antibiotics or hormones are given to them; and their beaks are not cut.

ANIMAL WELFARE APPROVED

Mainly used by family farms that raise chickens, this term indicates that the eggs come from farms that have been approved by Animal Welfare Approved, a group that strives to identify farms that produce food under the highest standards of animal welfare and environmental consciousness. Eggs with this label come from hens that have access to pasture and shelter, are fed a vegetarian diet, have not been given antibiotics, and have not had their beaks cut.

in quantity for egg production. Were geese or ducks or turkeys on par with chickens, their eggs might be what we go to the store to pick up a dozen of. It just so happens that the hen's egg seems to be the perfect size for our consumption; two make a meal, and one makes a portion when it's part of a meal, whether topping a *bibimbap* or as an integral part of pasta dough.

If ostrich eggs were all that was available, we'd be buying the egg in a different form. Quail eggs are popular and produced on a large scale, but they're so tiny as to be impractical for baking or making a custard—for anything, that is, that doesn't require their specific size. When I was in culinary school, we were rewarded with a quail egg and caviar pizza with Champagne if we'd performed well, an idea borrowed from Jeremiah Tower; the little quail egg fit perfectly on a single slice. They are the perfect hors d'oeuvre size—Thomas Keller serves a poached quail egg as a single bite on a gorgeous spoon, sauced with butter and a colorful garnish. I offer a different take on the quail egg canapé (page 34); it's decidedly showy but fun to prepare if you love to cook for guests.

Because we live near farms that raise ducks, we sometimes have access to duck eggs. If you do, too, please take advantage of them—they have big, rich yolks (see Poached Duck Egg on Duck Confit Hash, page 48).

The Whole Foods Market near us used to sell duck and ostrich eggs. Ostrich eggs are huge; if I had access to them, I'd probably scramble one, or make an omelet out of it. It would be a tricky size to fry or poach! But it will respond to heat and our palates pretty much the same way hens' eggs do. In this country we don't customarily raise turkeys to an egg-producing age unless they're specifically raised for making more turkeys.

There are, of course, fish eggs, which can be great to eat, but they, along with reptile eggs (eaten in certain parts of the world), are beyond the scope of this book, which is devoted to the mighty and ubiquitous hen's egg.

• • •

Part One

Egg / Whole

Cooked in Shell

The easiest way to cook an egg is to do so before removing it from its shell. It can be considered foolproof, as long as the eggs are roughly the same size and are cooked in water, which works the same no matter the kitchen or the equipment (though eggs may take a little longer at high altitudes). Some chefs recommend taking eggs out of the refrigerator an hour or two before cooking them to reduce the possibility of their cracking while cooking (puncturing the shell with a pin is said to do the same thing), but my own tests of this found little if any difference. Neither practice hurts the egg, but given that these acts have so little impact on the cooked egg, I don't find it practical.

You can also bake an egg in its shell to hard-cook it (20 minutes at 350°F/180°C) for the same result, but ovens differ and the heat is not nearly as uniform and dense as water, so again, baking eggs in their shell is impractical.

Eggs can be cooked in the ash of a fireplace, and there are numerous ancient recipes for this, but the temperature is inconsistent and thus the cooking uneven, often resulting in eggs that are overcooked and nasty tasting, so I don't recommend this except as a novelty method for the curious.

Interesting effects can be had by soaking peeled hard-cooked eggs in beet juice (pickled or not) or by lightly cracking the shells and immersing the eggs in tea to create a "shattered" pattern. Again, all well and good for those who like to play with food (indeed, something to be encouraged), but beyond my interests here, which are the practical matters of cooking eggs in their shell. Eggs can be cooked to varying degrees with a range of delicious, even dramatic results simply by using water in various ways.

• • •

Hard-Cooked

THE HARD-COOKED EGG

THE HARD-COOKED EGG IS AMONG THE simplest preparations of the egg. I love to eat them while they're still warm. I also love to eat them cold, with salt and pepper and a bite of cheese. They make a good start to the day, a quick fix when there's little time for lunch, and a satisfying canapé. I love deviled eggs, one of the great underused renditions of the egg (see page 209). And I love that old staple, egg salad. Finely chopped hard-cooked eggs make a fabulous garnish, sometimes called a mimosa (after the yellow flower). And they're also a critical component of the classic vinaigrette known as *sauce gribiche*. Hard-cooked eggs are so versatile, so easy, they're almost easy to overlook. But don't. They're too valuable.

HOW TO MAKE PERFECT HARD-COOKED EGGS

While it's the simplest and most routine of preparations, hard-cooking an egg can still be done carelessly, overcooked so that the white is rubbery and the yolk gray-green and sulfurous, or undercooked so that the yolk is uneven. On the other hand, when you cook it correctly and slice it open to see the beautifully uniform pastel yellow against the glossy white, it's something to delight in.

There is more than one way to hard-cook an egg, but the easiest and surest method is to use the uniform, dense, gentle heat of water, followed by water's powerful capacity to extract heat (an ice bath)—indeed, the most important part of the preparation is rapid cooling once they're done. The works-every-time method is this: put cold eggs in a pan in one layer, cover them with water by about 1 inch/2.5 centimeters, and put the pan over high heat. When the water comes to a full boil (at least 209°F/98°C), cover the pan, remove it from the heat, and let it sit for 15 minutes. Remove the eggs

to an ice bath (half ice, half water) until they're completely chilled, at least 10 minutes but preferably longer, giving the water a gentle stir every now and then to keep the cold circulating.

The result will be a uniformly yellow yolk, which indicates a perfectly cooked egg. If you overcook them or fail to chill them quickly and thoroughly, ferrous sulfide, with a gray-green color, the odor of sulfur, and an off flavor, can form on the surface of the yolk. If you undercook them, they may not look as pretty but they're still delicious. Peel and use the eggs right away, or store them in their shells in a covered container in the refrigerator for up to 2 weeks.

HARD-COOKED EGGS USING A PRESSURE COOKER

I have a pressure cooker, but I rarely use it. I am, however, frequently on Twitter (@ruhlman), where in the winter of 2012, someone asked me about pressure-cooking eggs. I replied that I had no experience, but asked anyone reading the feed to respond. Laura Pazzaglia (@hippressurecook), an American living in Italy, did. She said that pressure-cooking eggs was a brilliant method. I checked her profile and learned that she writes a blog called hippressurecooking.com. I was so intrigued I asked her to write a guest post for my site on pressure-cooking eggs, and she did.

After reading Laura's post and consulting other sources, I headed to the kitchen for my own highly scientific, exhaustive tests (two dozen eggs, a pressure cooker, and a stopwatch) to see for myself.

She's absolutely right. It's a fabulous way to cook eggs in the shell, primarily because it makes even the freshest eggs easy to peel. Fresh eggs have so little air in them that their shell and membrane tend to stick to the cooked egg white, forcing you

Overcooked

Perfectly cooked

Undercooked

to pull divots of white out of the egg as you peel it. A pressure cooker, however, creates a moisture barrier between the shell and the egg white so that the egg easily slips out of its shell. This is especially useful when you're making a lot of eggs, or when it's essential that the exterior of a hard-cooked egg remain pristine and smooth—that is, any time you won't be chopping up the egg for egg salad or for an egg garnish.

To hard-cook eggs using a pressure cooker, it's best to steam them, so you'll need a steamer basket or trivet to keep the eggs above the small amount of water in the pot.

1. Put the eggs in a steamer basket or on a trivet in the pot. Add 1 cup/240 milliliters water and lock the lid, turning the pressure setting to low. (Setting it to high usually results in violently cracked eggs.)

2. Put the pressure cooker over high heat. After the pressure button pops up, the steam will build and begin to whistle out of the valve. As soon as it reaches its maximum pitch, reduce the heat to medium-low and set your timer for 7 minutes.

3. Fill a large bowl with half ice and half water.

4. When 7 minutes have elapsed, remove the pot from the heat and allow it to cool to the point that the pressure button has fallen and you can open the pot. If after 5 minutes, the pressure button remains raised, run cold water over the pot until the pressure button drops.

5. Remove the eggs to the ice bath for at least 10 minutes, stirring the ice water a couple of times during the first minutes of cooling.

6. Peel and use the eggs right away, or store them in their shells in a covered container in the refrigerator for up to 2 weeks.

Times may vary by a minute depending on your cooker and your stove, so pay attention to initial results and adjust accordingly. For more on pressure-cooking eggs to different degrees of doneness, see page 15.

Egg Salad Three Ways

EGG SALAD IS ONE OF THE MOST ACCESSIBLE, easy, and delightful egg preparations, though the name confounds me. Why *salad*? Can't we come up with a better name for chopped eggs bound with mayonnaise? You can put it on lettuce if you want—but be sure it's crunchy lettuce, head lettuce or romaine, which serve as a serving vessel and garnish. Because egg salad is about the softest food you can make, it should always be paired with something crunchy: Toast. Crackers. Celery. Crisp bacon. Try making a lettuce wrap with the tarragon-chive version, or serve pappadams with the curried egg salad.

Egg salad rules of thumb:
*   2 eggs per serving
*   1 tablespoon mayonnaise per egg
*   judicious flavoring
    (herbs, spices, onion, as you wish)
*   crunch (croutons, celery)

I use a wooden bowl and a mezzaluna, a curved knife with a wooden handle, but a knife and cutting board work fine. If you want a smoother consistency, you can even use a food processor.

Egg salad is especially good when you make your own mayonnaise (Egg Salad with Homemade Lemon-Shallot Mayonnaise, page 9, is heaven to

1. / *A wooden bowl and a rounded knife called a mezzaluna are the perfect tools for quickly and neatly chopping hard-cooked eggs.*

4. / *Add the mayonnaise and the flavoring ingredients—here, chives, tarragon, and minced red onion.*

5. / *Continue to chop and mix the ingredients. If you haven't already done s give the eggs an aggressive dose of salt and several grinds of fresh pepper*

2. / *The yolks fall apart easily, so you mainly have to go after the whites.*

Chop the eggs to your taste. I like larger chunks of white, but those pictured here could be chopped even further for more uniformity.

me). And when you make your own mayonnaise, you can infuse the oil with intense flavors, as in the Curried Egg Salad (page 11), which also includes the aromatic flavors of garlic and ginger. But it's not essential, so wondrous are the fresh hard-cooked eggs themselves. And sometimes even I don't want to bother with homemade mayo (I always have some Hellmann's on hand for a fried-egg sandwich, page 31). In that case I make sure to load the eggs with plentiful, flavorful herbs, such as tarragon (my favorite herb with eggs) and the oniony chive.

I love an egg salad sandwich on toasted bread, but egg salad can also make an excellent—and elegant—canapé on crackers or small toasts, an hors d'oeuvre that can be made in advance. A tablespoonful on a water cracker garnished with a sprig of chervil or a small leaf of tarragon is a satisfying and economical bite to serve a lot of guests.

6. / *Egg salad ready to serve, on toast as a sandwich, on toast points as a canapé, or simply as is.*

Egg Salad with Tarragon and Chives

Egg Salad with Tarragon and Chives

SERVES 4 FOR SANDWICHES OR 12 FOR CANAPÉS

Tarragon is my favorite herb, both powerful and gentle, assertive yet delicate. It pairs beautifully with eggs. I also love the oniony punch of chives with egg. I make this as a summer lunch, when the herb garden is lush.

3 tablespoons minced red onion

Salt

8 hard-cooked eggs, peeled and coarsely chopped

Freshly ground black pepper

½ cup/120 milliliters Hellmann's mayonnaise (or, better yet, your own, page 161)

2 tablespoons chopped fresh tarragon

2 tablespoons minced fresh chives

Put the red onion in a small bowl and sprinkle liberally with salt, then cover with water for 5 to 10 minutes.

Put the eggs in a medium bowl. Give them a three- or four-finger dose of salt and a liberal application of freshly ground pepper. Add the mayonnaise. Strain the onion and add it, along with the herbs, and stir with a rubber spatula till all of the ingredients are uniformly combined.

Egg Salad with Homemade Lemon-Shallot Mayonnaise

SERVES 4 FOR SANDWICHES OR 12 FOR CANAPÉS

This is a rich delight made with your own homemade mayonnaise. I use a hand blender to make the mayonnaise quickly, which requires less muscle, but a whisk and a bowl work just as well. If the mayonnaise becomes too thick, add a few drops of water to thin it out.

8 hard-cooked eggs, peeled and coarsely chopped

Salt and freshly ground black pepper

2 celery ribs, cut into small dice

½ cup/120 milliliters Lemon-Shallot Mayonnaise (page 162)

Put the eggs in a medium bowl. Give them a three- or four-finger dose of salt and a liberal application of freshly ground pepper. Add the celery and the mayonnaise and stir with a rubber spatula until all of the ingredients are uniformly combined.

Curried Egg Salad

SERVES 4 FOR SANDWICHES OR 12 FOR CANAPÉS

Yes, you're allowed to put 2 teaspoons of raw curry powder into some store-bought mayonnaise and it will be fine, or even into your own mayonnaise, but what's the fun of that? Especially when you can ratchet up the taste by a factor of ten by making your own curried oil with ginger and garlic. In either event, buy a fresh jar of curry powder if you can't remember buying the one currently in your pantry. This mayonnaise can also be used to make excellent deviled eggs (page 209). I love to serve this in crunchy pappadams, pressed with a ladle into hot oil to give them a bowl shape.

FOR THE CURRIED MAYONNAISE:

¾ cup/180 milliliters vegetable oil

1 large garlic clove, minced

1 piece ginger (about ½ inch/1 centimeter long), peeled and finely grated

1 tablespoon good curry powder

½ teaspoon ground turmeric (optional)

Pinch of cayenne pepper

2 teaspoons fresh lime juice, plus more to taste

1 teaspoon water

½ teaspoon salt

1 egg yolk

FOR THE EGG SALAD:

¼ cup/25 grams minced red onion

Salt

8 hard-cooked eggs, peeled and coarsely chopped

2 celery ribs, cut into small dice

First, make the mayonnaise. Combine the oil, garlic, and ginger in a small sauté pan over high heat. When the garlic begins to simmer, reduce the heat to medium and continue cooking until the garlic is cooked (smell it; it should have lost its raw smell). Remove the pan from the heat and add the curry, turmeric (if using), and cayenne. Transfer the mixture to a glass measuring cup to cool.

While the oil is cooling, combine the lime juice, water, and salt in the vessel you'll be mixing your mayonnaise in and allow the salt to dissolve. Stir in the egg yolk. When the oil is cool enough to touch, emulsify it into the water-yolk mixture as you wish (see making mayonnaise, pages 160–61). Set the mayo aside. (It can be prepared and refrigerated in a covered container for up to 8 hours before mixing the salad.)

When you're ready to make the egg salad, put the red onion in a small bowl and sprinkle liberally with salt, then cover with water for 5 to 10 minutes.

Put the eggs in a medium bowl. Give them a three- or four-finger dose of salt. Strain the onion and add it, along with the celery and ½ cup/120 milliliters of the curried mayonnaise, and stir with a rubber spatula until all of the ingredients are uniformly incorporated.

Warm Hard-Cooked, Creamy-Yolk Egg with Ham and Cheddar

SERVES 1

When I was twenty, poor, and a solitary traveler in Amsterdam, I found myself lost and roomless in a seedy part of the city. I worked my way back to the tourist bureau near the train station, which directed me to a cheap B&B. It was dark by the time I found the right tram and the B&B, relieved just to be anywhere safe and dry. When I awoke in my tiny but clean, sun-lit room and went downstairs for breakfast, they had warm, hard-cooked eggs and cheese out on the counter. The day was cool and crystal clear. I found the warm eggs an uncommonly comforting and satisfying breakfast, especially with the rich, delicious cheese. My whole life I had eaten hard-cooked eggs chilly out of the fridge, and only on those rare occasions when we made them. So I associate warm, hard-cooked eggs and cheese with that long-ago trip, with unexpected safety and a crisp, bright day on friendly, foreign ground, where you discover something new about what had once seemed ordinary.

I like the yolk to be set in the center, but only just—dark yellow and creamy. Served with a hunk of cheese and a slice of good ham eaten by hand, it's a breakfast that lasts all day.

1 egg

1 demi-baguette, sliced in half lengthwise, then cut into the desired size for toast

A gratuitous amount of butter

1 (2-ounce/55-gram) chunk farmhouse cheddar

1 (2-ounce/55-gram) slab country ham

Put the egg in a pot covered with a couple inches of water. Bring the water to a boil over high heat, remove from the heat, and cover for 7 to 9 minutes.

Meanwhile, toast your bread, then butter it (with all other ingredients being dry, don't skimp!), and put it on a plate with the cheese and ham.

Remove the egg from the water and allow it to dry. Clip or peel the top of the egg as you wish. An eggcup and egg spoon are handy but not strictly necessary. Serve with the toast, cheese, and ham.

Soft-Cooked

THE SOFT-COOKED EGG

WHEN PREPARING EGGS IN THE SHELL, WE always want the white to be cooked, or at least somewhat opaque, but we don't always want the yolks cooked through. So it's good to have a handle on the range of egg donenesses available to you, from soft-cooked, in which the yolk is completely runny and the white just barely set; to what is called *mollet*, meaning that the white and part of the yolk are solid but the center of the yolk remains fluid; to just before fully hard-cooked, when the yolk is soft and creamy throughout but still slightly darker in the center than at the edge.

Eggs cooked so soft that the white remains somewhat runny should usually be eaten in the shell. An eggcup is the ideal serving piece, but you can also present a soft-cooked egg on a bed of kosher salt in a ramekin. Of course they're most commonly eaten for breakfast, with toast. But they're good anytime, and if for whatever reason you can't eat solid food, they're excellent, easy nutrition. In his lovely book *Eggs,* the Michelin-starred chef Michel Roux even suggests serving them as an elegant dessert, inviting guests to spoon caramel sauce into the liquid yolk at the table and dip *batonets* of brioche into the sweet yolky goodness.

Mollet eggs can be served as a garnish on, well, just about anything, but they're especially good on salads and on warm or room-temperature vegetables.

You'll notice differences in both flavor and texture from yolks cooked to varying nonliquid consistencies, so experiment until you find just the right combination.

To achieve across-the-board consistent results for the full range of egg donenesses, we again turn to the miracle tool, water, with its built-in thermometer and a density that makes it an enormously efficient heat giver.

Some cooks recommend starting with room-temperature eggs to reduce the chance of eggs cracking during the cooking, so feel free to remove your eggs from the fridge 1 to 2 hours before cooking them. I don't bother with this. First, it's not practical—I rarely remember to do it, or I don't even know in advance that I'm going to cook eggs. Second, I don't find that they cook any differently; whether the eggs started off cold or hot, my side-by-side trials were identical.

HOW TO MAKE PERFECT SOFT-COOKED EGGS

Put cold eggs in a pan in one layer, cover them with water by about 1 inch/2.5 centimeters, and put the pan over high heat. When the water reaches a full boil (at least 209°F/98°C), cover the pan, remove it from the heat, and follow the directions below for your preferred doneness.

For soft-cooked eggs: Remove the eggs from the water after 90 seconds if you want the whites to be loose, a true soft-cooked egg. For a soft-cooked egg in which the white is set but the yolk is molten, remove the egg after 3 minutes. Any time between 90 seconds and 3 minutes will yield a good soft-cooked egg. Cut the top off the eggshell and serve immediately.

For *mollet* eggs: Remove the eggs from the water after 5 to 7 minutes. At 5 minutes the yolk will be beginning to set, about ¼ inch/6 millimeters around the periphery, while the center remains molten. By 7 minutes, the center will be more solid than liquid but will be darker yellow and creamy. Either serve immediately or chill in an ice bath for

10 minutes and store in a covered container in the refrigerator for up to 2 days.

For fully cooked but creamy yolks: Remove the eggs from the water after 9 minutes. The white will be solid and the yolk will not be fluid, but rather dark and spreadable. Either serve immediately or chill in an ice bath for 10 minutes and store in a covered container in the refrigerator for up to 2 days.

SOFT-COOKED EGGS TO VARYING DONENESSES USING A PRESSURE COOKER

Pressure-cooking eggs is an ideal method if you want to serve soft-cooked eggs out of the shell, since it makes them so much easier to peel. As with pressure-cooking hard-cooked eggs (see page 5), you'll need a steamer basket or trivet to keep the eggs above the water in the pot.

1. Put the eggs in a steamer basket or on a trivet in the pot. Add 1 cup/240 milliliters water and lock the lid, turning the pressure setting to low. (Setting it to high usually results in violently cracked eggs.)

2. Put the pressure cooker over high heat. After the pressure button pops up, the steam will build and begin to whistle out of the valve. As soon as it reaches its maximum pitch, reduce the heat to medium-low and start your timer according to the next step.

3. For very soft eggs, cook for 3 minutes. For set whites and liquid yolks, 4 minutes will do (this will allow you to peel the egg without breaking it if you want to serve a whole egg out of the shell with a liquid yolk, as with the artichoke preparation on page 16). For medium-cooked eggs, cook for 5 minutes.

4. After the appropriate time, put the pot under cold running water until the pressure button falls (a few seconds). Release any remaining steam, open the pot, and serve the eggs or chill them in an ice bath (half ice, half water) for 10 minutes, depending on how you intend to serve the eggs. Soft-cooked eggs can be stored in a covered container in the refrigerator for up to 2 days.

Soft-Cooked Eggs on Artichoke Hearts with Creamy Lemon-Shallot Vinaigrette

SERVES 4

This dish pairs a classic thick lemon vinaigrette with artichoke, egg, and, for crunch and color, panko bread crumbs fried in butter. It is definitely in the Impress Your Date category of dishes and 80 percent guaranteed to work. Regardless, it's delicious and fun to eat, and each of the four components can be prepared well before serving (the mayonnaise should be made within hours of serving, but the artichoke and eggs can be cooked 2 days in advance if you wish). I also like mollet *eggs with this, but it's always impressive to have some yolk spill out when you cut into it, so they can be anywhere between soft and* mollet. *Serve some good toasted bread or extra-crispy fries with this. I serve this dish slightly warm, but it can be served cold or at room temperature, as you wish.*

4 whole artichokes

1 large onion, thinly sliced

Salt

4 eggs

1 to 2 tablespoons fresh lemon juice

1 cup/240 milliliters Lemon-Shallot Mayonnaise (page 162)

Pinch of cayenne pepper

¼ cup/10 grams minced fresh chives

¼ cup/20 grams panko, browned in 2 tablespoons butter (optional)

There are many ways to cook an artichoke, and any of them will work here. This way is the easiest and can be done a day or two ahead: Using a serrated knife, saw off the top half of each artichoke (this will make the leaves easier to remove after cooking) and cut the stem from the bottom so that it has a flat base. Stand the artichokes in a pot, scatter the sliced onion among them, and add enough water so that it comes halfway up the artichokes. Bring the water to a simmer over high heat, then reduce the heat to medium-low, cover the pot, and simmer until the artichokes are tender, 45 minutes to 1 hour. Transfer the artichokes to a plate to cool. When you can handle the artichokes comfortably, remove and discard the leaves and choke. Reserve the hearts and keep warm, or wrap and refrigerate them for up to 2 days.

Soft-cook the eggs to your desired doneness; pressure-cooking for 4 minutes is recommended for easy peeling, but the standard boil-and-cover, for a total cover time of 3 minutes, is fine, too. If you're not continuing with the recipe right away, chill the eggs in an ice bath for 10 minutes, then store in a covered container in the refrigerator for up to 2 days.

While the eggs are cooking, prepare the plates. Stir 1 tablespoon of the lemon juice into the mayonnaise and taste. It should be vinaigrette-strength to pair with the egg; add another tablespoon if you wish. Spoon 1 tablespoon mayonnaise into the center of each plate. Place an artichoke heart on top of the mayo (warm them in the microwave for 30 seconds if they were refrigerated). Spoon 2 tablespoons mayonnaise into the cup of the heart.

When the eggs are done, carefully peel them and place one on each artichoke. (If you've made the eggs ahead of time, first warm them in gently simmering water for 60 to 90 seconds.) Garnish with the cayenne, chives, and, if desired, the crunchy panko.

VARIATION: In the 1990s Cleveland chef Parker Bosley, one of the people who, in his own way, encouraged me to educate myself about food and cooking so I didn't continue to toil in ignorance, served a soft-cooked egg on spinach. It was the first time I'd had the surprise of cutting into what looked like a hard-cooked egg only to get the rush of bright yellow yolk spilling out onto the dark green spinach. Any kind of egg, from hard-cooked to poached, is great on spinach, but I loved the surprise of this preparation. When I next went to Parker's, I went back to the kitchen to ask the *chef de cuisine*, who did the actual cooking and peeling, how he peeled the soft-cooked eggs, as mine kept breaking when I tried it

at home. He shook his head wearily and said, "No secret, man, it's a real pain," with a gravitas that I knew implied, *and I can't wait till that damn dish is off the menu.*

Discovering the unique capacity of the pressure cooker to separate white from shell solved the problem (for the most part, anyhow—some eggs might break, so I always make extra; if they don't break, they can be refrigerated for a few more days and reheated or cooked further). If you want to try Parker's spinach version, replace the artichoke and vinaigrette with the spinach from the Shirred Eggs Florentine (page 42) and pressure-cook your egg for 4 minutes for easy peeling.

Pork Ramen with Soft-Cooked Egg and Scallions

SERVES 4

Hard-cooked eggs are common in ramen, but I particularly like soft-cooked eggs for this dish. They're easy to serve and come out perfectly every time.

Use a Japanese mandoline (often referred to as a Benriner, after the company that makes them) to julienne the vegetables; the radishes will look especially cool. You can use any pork and cook it any way you wish. Grilled over coals is best, but you can also roast it. I like using the pork skirt steak (from the diaphragm of the animal), which connects to the spareribs, and either roasting or grilling it before cooking it in the ramen for the flavor boost and for setting the protein. You can cook the pork whole, or slice and stir-fry it. If you are using pork shoulder, roasting it whole will make it easier to slice thinly. This is also a great way to use leftover pork.

It should go without saying that any meat and any good stock can be used in making this dish. Any tasty vegetables will work, too. Again, the key to excellence in this dish is a good stock and good noodles.

If you're using dried ramen noodles, you can cook them in the stock or precook them in salted water if you don't have enough stock.

1 quart/1 liter Pork Stock (recipe on facing page) or Miso-Kombu Broth (page 26)

Salt and freshly ground black pepper

1 pound/450 grams fresh ramen noodles (or 12 ounces/350 grams dried)

1 pound/450 grams cooked pork skirt steak or boneless pork shoulder, cut into ½-inch slices

4 eggs

8 ounces/225 grams baby spinach

2 carrots, peeled and julienned

4 radishes, julienned

6 scallions, sliced feather-thin on the diagonal

Put the stock in a large pot and bring it to a boil over high heat. Taste the stock and adjust the seasoning with salt and pepper if you wish. Add the ramen and cook for 1 minute, then add the pork and reduce the heat to low.

Put the eggs in a small pot and cover with water by about 1 inch/2.5 centimeters. Bring to a boil over high heat. Immediately cover the pot and remove it from the heat. Set a timer for 1 minute.

While the water is heating for the eggs, line four soup bowls with spinach. Divide the noodles, pork, and broth among the bowls. Garnish with the carrots, radishes, and scallions. Crack an egg into each bowl after they've sat in the covered pot for 1 minute, scraping out any white that may adhere to the shell. Serve immediately.

Pork Stock

MAKES 2 QUARTS/2 LITERS

It's important to roast or blanch any raw bones to avoid emulsifying the nasty coagulated protein that water pulls out of raw bones (for chicken stock it's enough to skim the stock once it's come to a simmer). Any pork bones with lots of connective tissue and meat, such as neck bones or joints, will do. I like to use pigs' feet because they have an abundance of all the stuff you need for great stock: meat for flavor and bones and skin for body (skin has a lot of gelatin, which is where the body comes from). They make for a very earthy, farmlike pork broth.

4 pigs' feet or 2 pounds/910 grams meaty pork bones and joints

2 Spanish onions, roughly chopped

4 carrots, roughly chopped

4 celery ribs

5 garlic cloves

¼ cup/70 grams tomato paste

2 bay leaves

2 teaspoons whole black peppercorns, roughly chopped or coarsely ground in a mortar and pestle

Several parsley sprigs (optional)

Put the pigs' feet in a pot that will hold them and allow you to cover them by a couple of inches of water (but not so big that you have to add too much water; a general rule is 2 parts bones, 3 parts water by weight). Turn the heat to high. When the water reaches a boil, strain the pork bones, and rinse them in cold water. Wipe out the pot, return the bones to it, and add water until they are covered by a couple of inches. Bring the water to a simmer. Now you can either turn the heat to low and let it cook, uncovered, for 8 to 10 hours or, better, put it in the oven, uncovered, set to its lowest setting overnight.

After the stock has cooked for at least 8 (and as many as 12) hours, add the remaining ingredients. Bring the stock back to a simmer on the stovetop, then turn the heat to low and cook for another hour or so.

Pass the stock through a fine-mesh strainer. For an even more refined stock, strain it again through cheesecloth.

This will make twice what you need for the pork ramen recipe; the rest can be stored in a covered container in the refrigerator for up to 4 days or in the freezer for up to 3 months.

Soft-Cooked Egg with Buttered Toast for Two

SERVES 2

My grandma once served me a soft-cooked egg by pouring and scraping it from the shell into a bowl. It looked disgusting and I'll never forget it. But there is something comforting and visually appealing about eating a very soft egg straight from the shell, and enjoying it with that other simple preparation, buttered toast. Toast made from grocery-store sandwich bread has no flavor, so I recommend using a slice of sourdough bread. I prefer to toast the bread twice. First dry, then buttered so that the butter is bubbling hot and flavorful when you serve it. You'll need eggcups and egg spoons to serve.

I see this being eaten on a Sunday morning after a happily drunken Saturday night, freshly showered and shaved and in a smoking jacket that I'd like to own, across from my equally contented wife, each of us reading the Times and pretending that all is well with the world. (Consider serving with a Bloody Mary, depending on how useless you're willing to be for the rest of the day.)

2 slices sourdough bread or good country bread

2 eggs

A gratuitous amount of butter

Abundant strong coffee, preferably a full fresh percolator

2 Bloody Marys (optional)

Toast the bread.

Meanwhile, cover your eggs with 2 inches/ 5 centimeters water in a small saucepan. Bring the water to a boil over high heat. Remove from the heat and cover for 2 to 3 minutes (I think 3 is perfect, but 2 will give you a truly soft-cooked egg).

While your water is boiling, butter your toast and retoast till the butter is bubbling.

Kiss your spouse's crown and say, "Love you."

Transfer the eggs from the water to the eggcups, slice off the top ½ inch/1 centimeter with an egg cutter or knife, and serve with the toast and hot coffee, followed by a Bloody Mary, if desired.

Mollet

Crispy Mollet Egg with Asparagus

SERVES 4

I often use this asparagus sauce garnished with asparagus tips for sautéed scallops, a great pairing. But it works beautifully with egg as well. I love the crispy egg preparation here, simply breaded and fried. I think a mollet *egg is best, but feel free to do a soft-cooked egg as for the Soft-Cooked Eggs on Artichoke Hearts (page 16). Both the asparagus and eggs can be cooked the day before serving.*

1 pound/450 grams asparagus, woody ends trimmed

5 eggs

2 tablespoons minced shallot

2 tablespoons fresh lemon juice

About ½ cup flour

About 1 cup panko

Vegetable oil for deep-frying

¼ cup/60 grams butter, cut into 3 pieces

Salt

Grated lemon zest (optional)

Bring a large pot of heavily salted water to a boil and cook the asparagus in it till tender, a few minutes (taste one to see if it's done). Drain and plunge them into an ice bath (half ice, half water) till thoroughly chilled, then drain again.

Cut off the asparagus tips and reserve in a small dish covered with a damp paper towel and plastic wrap. Cut the stems into 1-inch/2.5-centimeter pieces and puree in a blender, adding just enough cold water or ice to get the pieces spinning. Cover and keep refrigerated till you're ready to finish the dish.

Cook all but one of the eggs to the *mollet* stage (boil for 5 minutes, page 14, or use the pressure cooker method, page 15) and chill in an ice bath. Carefully peel them (this will be easier if you used the pressure cooker).

Meanwhile, combine the shallot and lemon juice in a small bowl and set aside.

Whisk the remaining egg in a shallow dish till it's uniformly mixed. Put the flour in a plastic bag and the panko in a bowl.

Carefully dredge the peeled eggs in the flour, then roll them in the beaten egg until the flour has absorbed it, then roll them in the panko, where they can stay till you're ready to cook them.

Heat 3 inches/7.5 centimeters oil in a high-sided saucepan over high heat. When the oil is hot, drop in the eggs. Cook until browned, 2 to 3 minutes. (Alternatively, you can pan-fry the eggs, with the oil coming halfway up the eggs, turning them till golden brown, 2 to 3 minutes.) Use a slotted spoon to transfer the crispy eggs to a plate.

Put the asparagus sauce in a small saucepan over medium-high heat. When it begins to bubble, reduce the heat to medium and add the butter pieces one at a time, whisking continuously until the butter is melted. Season the sauce with salt and remove it from the heat.

Reheat the asparagus tips in the microwave for 20 or 30 seconds.

Divide the sauce among four plates. Strain the shallot and sprinkle on top of the sauce on each plate. Scatter the asparagus tips along the periphery of the sauce. Place an egg on each plate, grate some lemon zest over the dish, if desired, and serve.

Sous Vide

COOKING EGGS *SOUS VIDE*

WHILE *SOUS VIDE* LITERALLY TRANSLATES as "under vacuum," referring to vacuum-sealed food cooked in water at precise, below-boiling temperatures, we use the term *sous vide* broadly to indicate the cooking of *any* food at precise, below-boiling temperatures.

The devices used to maintain exact temperatures, immersion circulators and *sous vide* water-bath systems, have been used in restaurant kitchens for some time and are now becoming affordable enough that they are found in home kitchens as well.

Eggs, already packaged by nature and ready for water, are fun to cook *sous vide* because you can create textures in both the yolk and the white that are otherwise impossible to achieve. If you cook them at 144.5°F/62.5°C for 35 to 45 minutes, you will have a perfect soft-cooked-like egg that can finish cooking in a hot broth: the white will be quiveringly tender, with most of the proteins fully congealed and others just barely opaque, and the yolk warm but fluid. This is the perfect way to cook an egg that will be served as a garnish in another dish. It's great for entertaining since you can do a lot of eggs at once and they all come out perfect; they're also easy to serve since they more or less pour out of the shell. So these can be used in virtually any soup or stew, on hot grits, or with slow-cooked beans.

Ramen is the perfect vehicle for a soft-cooked egg. Because there are two ramen recipes here, one pork-based and one vegetarian, I'm recommending two different methods for soft-cooked eggs, one cooked as a regular soft-boiled egg and one cooked *sous vide* for those who have *sous vide* equipment. In both dishes the egg finishes cooking in the stock, so either egg-cooking method can be used in either recipe.

Ramen with Soft-Cooked Eggs

RAMEN, THE JAPANESE NOODLE, HAS BEEN largely debased in America by packaged dry ramen with nasty "flavoring" packets. Great ramen has a distinctive flavor due to alkaline (as opposed to acidic) ingredients, such as sodium and/or potassium carbonate, food-grade lye, or even baking soda. If you live in a city that offers fresh ramen, it's worth seeking it out. If you like to make pasta at home, the recipes in David Chang's *Momofuku* cookbook or Takashi Yagihashi's *Noodles* are worth the effort. But you can also use the packaged ramen sold in every grocery store—the noodles themselves are fine, it's the flavoring packets that are just plain wrong in every way.

I'm offering two versions, one with pork because I love all things pork, and a vegetarian ramen dish made simply with onion and miso, no elaborate stock-making required.

The real star here is the soft-cooked egg added to the soup at the end. If you have an immersion circulator or *sous vide* water bath, cook your egg at 144.5°F/62.5°C for 45 minutes. If you don't, you can get a similar effect by bringing a large pot of water to 150°F/65°C, removing it from the heat, putting your eggs in the water, covering the pot, and letting the eggs cook in the hot water, undisturbed, for 45 minutes.

Ramen is a great dish because you can do anything you want with it, give it any garnish, seasoning, or spice you want (just don't use that horrible mixture of flavored salt they put in the package!). Of course it's best when you make your own stock, because good stock is one of those things that you cannot buy at a store. Small amounts of stock are not difficult to make, and the vegetarian ramen recipe here uses a ridiculously simple concoction that can't even be called stock it's so easy.

The basic ramen recipe is simple: Heat up 1 quart/1 liter stock. Add 1 pound/450 grams fresh ramen. Add any garnish that needs cooking (such as meat or hard vegetables), then serve, garnished as you wish with scallions, mushrooms, bamboo shoots, and an egg, of course.

Ramen with Miso-Kombu Broth, Shiitake Mushrooms, and Sous Vide Egg

SERVES 4

This is a light, refreshing vegetarian ramen dish. I like to sear the shiitakes in a very lightly oiled cast-iron pan to brown them and intensify their flavor, but they can also simply be sliced and added to the broth raw. Save the stems to add to the Miso-Kombu Broth.

4 eggs

1 quart/1 liter Miso-Kombu Broth (recipe below)

1 pound/450 grams fresh ramen noodles (or 12 ounces/350 grams dried)

¼ pound/115 grams fresh shiitake mushrooms (approximately 20), stems removed, caps sliced and sautéed, roasted, or raw

6 scallions, sliced feather-thin on the diagonal

2 carrots, peeled and julienned

4 radishes, julienned

Preheat a *sous vide* water bath to 144.5°F/62.5°C and add the eggs.

Shortly before the eggs are done (they should be in the water bath for at least 35 minutes and as long as 45 minutes), bring the broth to a simmer in a large pot. Add the ramen noodles and cook till they're done. Divide the broth and noodles among four bowls. Garnish with the shiitakes, scallions, carrots, and radishes.

Crack one egg into each bowl of broth. Serve immediately.

Miso-Kombu Broth

MAKES 1 QUART/1 LITER

This is a delicious, simple broth, not unlike miso soup. You can use white, red, or mixed miso, whatever kind you prefer. I use white, or shiro, miso. Kombu seaweed and bonito flakes are both available at Asian markets and some grocery stores. They give the broth a fresh-sea flavor, but you can omit them or substitute fish sauce for a different but not dissimilar effect. The kombu may have blooms of chalky, salty minerals—this is good stuff, so don't rinse it off. The broth should be cooked very gently, steeped rather than simmered.

1 quart/1 liter water

1 Spanish onion, roughly chopped

½ ounce/15 grams kombu (1 or 2 large sheets)

Leftover shiitake stems (optional)

1 ounce/25 grams bonito flakes (about 1 cup)

2 tablespoons miso paste

Pour the water into a large pot and add the onion. Bring the water to a simmer over high heat, then reduce the heat to low. Add the kombu and mushroom stems (if using) and cook for 1 hour. Stir in the bonito flakes and cook for another 5 minutes. Stir in the miso. When it has dispersed, pass the stock through a fine-mesh strainer into a clean vessel. Use as desired, or store in a covered container in the refrigerator for up to 1 day or in the freezer for up to 2 months.

Part Two

Egg / Whole

Cooked out of Shell

Once we remove the egg from its lovely walls, we can have even more fun, depending on what our final goals are. We can cook it in dry heat or wet heat; high-high heat or gentle heat; free-form or in a mold; with yolk and white distinct, uniformly blended, or even in between, as with the first preparation here.

• • •

Gently Fried

Weekend Broken-Yolk Fried-Egg Sandwich

SERVES 1 HURRIED FATHER, MOTHER, OR FIFTH-GRADER

Here eggs are gently fried in butter before all of the water has cooked out of the butter, so that they are cooking at near poaching temperatures. Cooking eggs gently will render them very tender and mildly flavored. If you heat a steel pan properly, and that pan is pristine, and you allow the butter to melt and wait until the bubbling is just beginning to subside, your eggs should not stick. But sometimes they do stick, and then you wind up with a scrambled-egg sandwich, which is OK but not as good. So, if you have a good nonstick pan, this is one of the few times to put it to use. (As a rule, cooking with nonstick pans should be avoided, as they don't allow you to develop the best browning, which is where the flavor comes from. They're always the best choice for eggs when cooking with low heat, however.)

I've been making fried-egg sandwiches since I was in fifth grade, and they remain a common, quick lunch, especially on a Saturday when I've got a lot of errands or projects to get done. It's quick and satisfying, and lasts me all day.

I have a reputation for advising people to avoid processed food, like making BLTs completely from scratch, for instance: curing your own bacon, growing the lettuce and tomato, baking the bread, and so on. So a lot of people are surprised when I tell them that I keep a jar of Hellmann's mayonnaise in our fridge. I love Hellmann's, and there's nothing wrong with using it as long as you recognize that homemade mayo is a completely different product. You make home-made mayonnaise in part because you can't buy mayonnaise of the quality you can make at home.

But on a busy Saturday, if I've got a long To Do list, I'm not going to take an extra 5 minutes to make mayonnaise; I'll have a quick fried-egg sandwich, with Hellmann's, on soft sandwich bread, and a glass of milk. If you want to make your own mayo, go to town; instructions are on pages 160–61 and you will be rewarded with a superlative *egg sandwich.*

I break the yolk before adding it to the pan so that it intermingles with the white as it cooks, which of course is part of the unique flavor of eggs cooked this way.

1 tablespoon butter

2 eggs, cracked into a bowl, yolks poked once to break them

Salt and freshly ground black pepper to taste

Mayonnaise

2 pieces soft sandwich bread

Put a pan (preferably nonstick) over medium-low heat and allow it to get hot, about 5 minutes. Add the butter and allow it to melt completely. As the water cooks out of it, it will froth. When the frothing seems to be at its peak, pour in the eggs and give the pan an immediate shake to prevent the eggs from sticking. Season the eggs with salt and pepper and cook for 1 minute. Flip the eggs and cook until the white is just set, about 1 minute more.

Meanwhile, spread as much or as little mayonnaise on the sandwich bread as you wish. When the eggs are done, pour them out onto the bread, folding them over so that the eggs don't flop over the edges of the bread. Cover the eggs with the other piece of bread and eat with a glass of milk. I usually eat right there next to the stove, don't even use a plate.

Gently Fried Eggs on Grits with Bacon and Toast

SERVES 4

This is by far one of my favorite breakfasts, taking advantage of a seriously underused food, grits, which is coarsely ground corn. (Corn kernels treated with an alkaline solution and ground are called hominy grits.) Grits alone are wonderful, but something magical happens when egg yolk runs through them.

I include this recipe not only to contrast a gently fried egg with an egg fried in superhot oil, but also as an excuse to encourage people to eat a delicacy rarely served outside of America's southern states. Please don't use instant grits, and it's worth mail-ordering very good grits such as those offered by Anson Mills, McEwen & Sons, or Adluh Flour.

Grits should be creamy. The amount of liquid needed varies depending on how long you cook the grits, so use your common sense; you can't really overcook them. Cheese pairs beautifully with grits as an enricher; cheddar is common, but a Nashville friend is devoted to smoked Gouda in grits. Makes me hungry just thinking about it.

1 quart/1 liter water

1 cup/170 grams grits

2 cups/480 milliliters milk

Salt and freshly ground pepper

6 tablespoons/90 grams butter, plus more for the toast

½ cup/60 grams shredded cheddar cheese (optional)

8 slices bacon

4 slices bread

4 eggs

Combine the water and grits in a medium saucepan, bring to a simmer over high heat, and reduce the heat to low. Cook, stirring frequently, to the consistency you prefer, loose or stiff. Most grits will be done in 30 to 40 minutes, but they can be cooked slowly for many hours—just add more liquid as needed. To finish the grits, add as much of the milk as needed and plenty of salt and pepper. Stir in 4 tablespoons/60 grams of the butter, or more if you wish, taste again, and add more salt if necessary. Continue cooking till the consistency is to your liking and stir in the cheese just before serving.

While the grits are finishing, fry the bacon in a pan (I like to start the bacon in ½ cup water, which begins the rendering process). When the bacon is done, drain it on paper towels. Toast the bread.

Melt the remaining 2 tablespoons/30 grams butter in a large, nonstick pan over medium heat. Crack the eggs into the pan. For eggs sunny-side up, cover the pan and cook just until set, a few minutes. If you want them over easy, don't cover the pan, and flip the eggs after a few minutes, before the white is set. Meanwhile, butter the toast and place a mound of grits on each plate.

Top each mound of grits with a fried egg and serve with toast and bacon.

Quail Eggs Croque Madame

MAKES 12 CANAPÉS

Quail eggs are perfect for show-offy canapés and can be prepared in numerous ways. My first taste of this delicacy was in culinary school, when chef-instructor Ron DeSantis rewarded us with a quail egg and caviar pizza after a good run at the St. Andrew's Café on graduation day (an idea he took outright, he told our class, from Jeremiah Tower, who made it popular at Stars in San Francisco). I had my next quail egg in the kitchen of the French Laundry, where Thomas Keller poached them before service, then reheated them in a little butter and garnish and served them on silver spoons as a fun one-bite course. When I found some in Cleveland I wrote about them on my blog, frying them and serving them on a spoon with some wilted arugula, bacon, and English muffin croutons. You could easily lose the arugula and poach the eggs and serve them as eggs Benedict canapés. Or you can go all out and make this take on the croque madame: *grilled ham and cheese with Mornay sauce and a fried egg on top, one of my favorite meals.*

FOR THE MORNAY SAUCE:

1 tablespoon butter

1 shallot, minced

Salt and freshly ground black pepper to taste

1½ tablespoons flour

1 cup/240 milliliters milk

A few gratings of fresh nutmeg

¼ cup/130 grams grated Gruyère or Emmentaler cheese

FOR THE CROQUE MADAME:

12 slices mini sandwich bread or any thinly sliced bread cut into 2-inch/5-centimeter rounds

1 to 2 tablespoons Dijon mustard

6 ounces/170 grams ham, julienned, at room temperature

4 teaspoons/40 grams grated Gruyère or Emmentaler cheese

1 tablespoon butter

12 quail eggs

***Fleur de sel* or coarse sea salt**

Preheat the broiler.

To make the Mornay sauce, combine the butter and the shallot in a small saucepan over medium heat. Season the shallot with a good pinch of salt and a few grinds of pepper. Cook until the shallot is tender, a couple of minutes, then add the flour and cook, stirring, for another minute. Whisk in the milk and bring to a simmer to thicken the milk. Turn the heat to low and grate in some nutmeg, then stir in the cheese. Set aside.

To make the croque madame, lightly toast the bread rounds. Spread thinly with the Dijon. Top each with some of the ham and the cheese. Gently broil to melt the cheese.

Reheat the sauce over low heat. Heat the butter in one or two nonstick sauté pans over medium heat. When the cheese on the croutons is melted, crack the eggs into the pan(s) and cover.

Place the croutons on a platter and spoon a bit of sauce on each. When the eggs are cooked (sunny-side up takes just a few minutes), place one on each crouton and garnish with *fleur de sel* or coarse salt. Serve immediately.

Aggressively Fried

<hr>

Michael Pardus's Bibimbap

SERVES 4

When I was reporting The Reach of a Chef, *I spent some time with my old skills instructor and friend Michael Pardus, who was by then teaching Asian cuisines. It was Korea Day when I cooked there, and for a kind of extra-credit dish he'd assigned us something called* bibimbap, *which translates more or less as "thrown together with rice." A* bibimbap *can be a clean-out-the-fridge dish, but Pardus used marinated skirt steak and vegetables and topped it with a fried egg, which is not uncommon. (As you can see from many of the recipes in the whole-egg section, there are very few dishes that aren't improved by the addition of an egg.)*

It was the eggs that gave me a bit of a problem during service. They kept sticking and breaking. While I was charged with making only ten of them, it was a complete disaster. Bibimbap *had handed me my ass. But it made me think about the sticking issue. I eventually figured out that sticking is not an issue in a steel pan if you get it smoking hot. This also results in the egg white becoming brown and crispy and flavorful, which I don't want in my sandwich, but I very much want in my* bibimbap. *This simple, delicious preparation has become a staple meal in our house.*

A NOTE ABOUT THE BEEF: *I think it's best to julienne the beef, but depending on the size and cut you use, you can simply slice it as thinly as possible; if you want to cut these slices in half, that's fine. If you use flank steak, cut across the grain; if using skirt, cut with the grain along the natural striations; in either case, you'll be cutting widthwise, not lengthwise.*

FOR THE MARINATED BEEF:

1 pound/450 grams beef skirt steak or flank steak, sliced as desired

2 scallions, finely sliced

2 garlic cloves, smashed aggressively with the flat side of a knife and roughly chopped

1 tablespoon peeled and grated fresh ginger

2 tablespoons soy sauce

1 teaspoon sugar

FOR THE KOREAN RED PEPPER SAUCE:

2 tablespoons gochujang or other Korean red pepper paste

2 tablespoons water

2 teaspoons rice vinegar

1 teaspoon sugar

1 teaspoon fish sauce

1 teaspoon toasted sesame oil

FOR THE BIBIMBAP:

1½ cups/280 grams jasmine rice, well rinsed

¼ cup/60 milliliters vegetable oil

½ cup/100 grams peeled, julienned carrot

½ cup/100 grams julienned daikon radish

½ cup/100 grams julienned celery

½ cup/100 grams julienned head lettuce

4 eggs, each cracked into its own ramekin

Combine the sliced beef and other marinade ingredients in a covered container or zipper-top plastic bag and marinate in the refrigerator for up to 48 hours (optimally you'll want to give the meat at least 1 hour to marinate, but if you just got home from work, don't sweat the marinating time.)

In a small bowl, stir together all of the ingredients for the red pepper sauce and set aside.

Put the rice in a medium saucepan and cover it with about 1 inch/2.5 centimeters water. Put the pan over high heat and boil the rice till the water has reached the level of the rice and the steam holes are releasing bubbles (aka "fish eyes"). Cover the pot and put it on a back burner over low heat.

Put a wok over high heat. Put a large sauté pan with a cover over low heat. When the wok is smoking hot, add 2 tablespoons/30 milliliters of the vegetable oil and allow it to get smoking hot. Add the beef and stir-fry until cooked, 2 minutes or so. Add the red pepper sauce and stir to combine.

Turn the burner with the sauté pan to high.

Add the vegetables to the beef in the wok, turn the heat off, and stir to combine.

When the sauté pan is hot, add the remaining 2 tablespoons/30 milliliters vegetable oil and allow it to get almost smoking. Quickly pour in the eggs, one at a time, leaving space between them, and allow them to cook for 20 seconds or so, then cover the pan and reduce the heat to low.

Divide the rice among four large bowls. Top with the beef and vegetables. When the whites of the eggs have congealed but the yolks are still fluid, place an egg atop the beef and vegetables in each bowl. Serve immediately.

Deep Fried

Frisée Salad with Bacon Vinaigrette and Deep-Fried Egg

SERVES 4

Yes, you can crack eggs into boiling oil and in about 15 or 20 seconds have a fabulous egg, with cooked whites and a runny yolk. It doesn't look or taste oily at all, and the high heat makes some of the white turn brown and crispy—if you're lucky, you may even get a crisp comet tail on it (page 29). This egg could go in any of the preceding recipes, but because you're deep-frying, you should pair it with something acidic. I like to put it on a bed of frisée lettuce, which is slightly bitter and chewy-crunchy, and for a little extra flavor, bacon bits, for a different take on the French lardon salad. Use the paler parts of the frisée, which are a little less bitter. Add a few drops of red wine vinegar and maybe a dot or three of balsamic to offset the pleasant bitterness of the greens and you're good to go. This makes an impressive opening course for a bigger dinner or the perfect light lunch. The bacon can be cooked well in advance of serving if you wish, but save the fat in the pan for coating the frisée.

3 ounces/85 grams sliced bacon (2 extra-thick slices)

Vegetable oil for deep-frying (2 to 3 cups/480 to 720 milliliters)

8 ounces/225 grams frisée lettuce

1 teaspoon red wine vinegar

Balsamic vinegar

Salt and freshly ground black pepper

4 eggs, each cracked into its own ramekin

In a medium sauté pan or cast-iron skillet, sauté the bacon till it's crispy.

While the bacon is cooking, get the oil heating in a medium high-sided saucepan or, better, a wok, the shape of which allows you to use less cooking oil.

Chop the crispy bacon into bits. Pour off all but about 1 tablespoon of the fat from the pan the bacon cooked in. Return the bacon to the pan. Toss the frisée in the pan to lightly coat the lettuce with the fat (it's fine if the pan is still hot), then divide among four plates. Scatter any bacon bits left in the pan on the salads.

Sprinkle about ¼ teaspoon of the red wine vinegar over each salad, or more to taste, and a few dots of balsamic around the edges of the plates. Season to taste with salt and pepper.

Line a plate with paper towels for the eggs. When the oil reaches 375°F/190°C (or when a chopstick bubbles vigorously when inserted into the oil, but before the oil begins to smoke), pour each egg into the oil and cook, stirring the oil gently; the eggs will sink, then float. Flip them if they'll let you, or spoon oil over their tops until the whites are set, 15 or 20 seconds total. Use a slotted spoon to remove them to the paper towels to drain for a moment (try to remove the eggs in the same order they were added to the oil). Sprinkle them with a little salt, then place each atop a salad and serve immediately.

Coddled

JUST THE SOUND OF THIS PREPARATION, coddled egg, comforts. *Coddle* means to treat tenderly, and the word may derive from *caudle*, a warm drink for invalids. And so a coddled egg is treated as if it were a culinary invalid. Of course, it is a culinary superhero, but here we handle it with the utmost gentleness, protected on all sides from heat, the gentlest of heat, in a covered container. (There's some disagreement on just what coddled eggs are. Some culinary authors, including James Beard and Madeleine Kamman, write that a coddled egg is cooked in the shell for a short time. But others, such as myself, call this a soft-cooked egg. I believe we should use the term *coddle* solely to describe an egg gently cooked out of the shell, in a covered vessel.) While coddled eggs are certainly a restorative nourishment, they should in no way be limited to invalids. Indeed, it is an uncommonly elegant preparation, delicious, and virtually foolproof.

Because it's relatively uncommon, I find it to be a wonderful breakfast for weekend guests. It's also something of a no-brainer—10 to 12 minutes in hot water does the trick.

The egg alone is fine, but it should be flavored somehow. When I was considering the many possible ways, refrigerator door open, scanning its contents for ideas, my eyes stopped on a small plastic container of butter flavored with black truffles. Butter and eggs, truffle and eggs—no more felicitous pairings on earth. And it would be so simple. Crack an egg into the coddler, add a dollop of truffle butter, cover it, and put it in a water bath, just until the white is set. Season with a little *fleur de sel* or Maldon salt, re-cover, and serve with some toast. I like to make batons of toast that I can dip into the yolk.

I remembered that Thomas Keller's Manhattan restaurant Per Se serves a coddled egg. I wrote to one of its managers, fellow Cleveland native Michael Minnillo, to ask how they serve it. He wrote back, "Just a little truffle butter." I should have known! I also asked what they serve it in, as I'd asked Donna, photographer in charge of props, to find some nice coddlers. Michael emailed a link to their coddler, I forwarded it to Donna, and she, in the next room, shouted out immediately, "That's one of the coddlers I've ordered!" I guess our long association with Thomas Keller and his restaurants has left its mark.

While truffle butter is exquisite and easy, it's by no means the only flavoring you could use. A teaspoon of cream and some tarragon would be lovely. Several drops of excellent extra-virgin olive oil and Parmigiano-Reggiano is delicious. I'm not a fan of hot sauce on eggs, but a shot of sriracha would be great if your palate demands some heat.

Coddled eggs must be cooked in a water bath, 10 minutes for loose white, 12 to 15 minutes for a firmer egg. The time will vary depending on the thickness of the vessel, so determine doneness by looking at the egg. Buy coddlers if you want to emulate Martha Stewart, but you can also coddle eggs in a ramekin loosely covered with foil or even in demitasse coffee cups. That would be quite elegant, actually. Maybe that wedding-gift china will get a little more use around our house now that I've thought of this.

Coddled Eggs with Truffle Butter

SERVES 4

4 eggs

4 teaspoons black truffle butter
(or other flavorings as noted above)

Fleur de sel, gray salt, or Maldon salt

Freshly ground pepper

Preheat the oven to 300°F/150°C.

Bring a pot of water to a boil—the amount will be determined by the size of your water-bath vessel and coddlers.

Crack an egg into each coddler, add a teaspoon of truffle butter, and cover. Put the coddlers in a baking dish or high-sided pan. Pour boiling water into the dish so that it reaches the level of the egg or even goes above it, taking care not to get any water in the coddlers.

Place the baking dish in the oven and coddle the eggs until they are the way you like them, 10 to 15 minutes. Serve immediately.

Shirred

SHIRRED EGGS ARE BAKED USING DIRECT heat, as opposed to coddled eggs, which use the gentle heat of water in the form of a water bath on the outside and steam trapped within the coddler. They're equally comforting and equally delicious, but the flavors take on a bit more complexity due to the high heat and added ingredients. I think a little cream or butter makes a sweet addition. Freshly grated Parmigiano-Reggiano is an excellent finish and, slightly browned beneath a broiler, contributes color as well as flavor.

If you want to add other elements, there's no end to what you might use. You could go traditional and line the ramekin with cooked spinach, sautéed shiitake mushrooms, roasted red bell pepper, or broiled eggplant. You could add ham or bacon or duck confit. Some minced shallot cooked in a little butter is always a delicious addition.

As far as technique goes, the egg cooks a little more evenly if you heat the ramekin in a microwave, on the stove top, or in the oven first. Bake the eggs in a 350°F/180°C oven just till they're set, about 10 minutes. You can also broil them, if you wish—a good strategy if you're topping the eggs with cheese.

The size of the shirring vessel is critical—it should be wide and shallow, not a conventional round ramekin. A standard 8-ounce/240-milliliter round ramekin can be used to shirr 1 egg, but 2 eggs would be best cooked in a water bath for triple the time to ensure good texture throughout (a shirr/coddle combination).

Shirred Eggs Florentine for My Mom

SERVES 1 MOM AND 1 SON

My mom loves shirred eggs with spinach, but she was having trouble perfecting the preparation, so this recipe is for her. You can cook the spinach either by blanching it and then shocking it in an ice bath, or by sautéing it in butter with some shallots (my preference). Either way, wring it out and chop it before adding it to the ramekins.

2 teaspoons butter

8 ounces/225 grams spinach, cooked, thoroughly squeezed dry, coarsely chopped

4 eggs

2 tablespoons heavy cream

Salt and freshly ground black pepper

Several gratings of Parmigiano-Reggiano

Good buttered toast

Preheat the oven to 350°F/180°C.

Put 1 teaspoon butter in each of two shallow ramekins or shirring dishes. Divide the cooked spinach between the two ramekins. Heat the ramekins in a microwave so that the spinach is hot but the ramekin is not too hot to hold, 30 to 40 seconds.

Crack 2 eggs into each ramekin, add 1 tablespoon cream to each, and season to taste with salt and pepper. Sprinkle some cheese over the eggs.

Put the ramekins in the oven and cook until the whites have fully congealed, 10 to 15 minutes. Serve with toast.

EGGS FLORENTINE

1. / *Be sure the spinach and ramekins are gently heated before adding the eggs.*

2. / *Finish the eggs with grated cheese, pop them in the oven, and cook them until they are beautiful.*

Poached in Water

POACHING AN EGG IN WATER IS INSTRUCTIVE in the ways of the egg. In particular, it provides a dramatic display of the different parts of the egg white. While an egg white comprises several different proteins that coagulate at different temperatures, there are two visible parts of the white, the loose part and the thicker, more cohesive part. Crack an egg onto a plate and see for yourself. Usually, the fresher the egg, the more of the thicker part of the white there will be, and the thicker it will be.

The poached egg is one of the simplest, most versatile of all egg preparations. The white cooks faster than the fat-rich yolk, and the gentle heat of the water keeps the white tender. It is also infinitely variable. Just check out the list of variations on the "Eggs Benedict" page in Wikipedia—more than twenty—and those are just the most common ones. On toast, on an artichoke heart, on polenta, on a crab cake, on a *lardon* salad, in a soup—there's pretty much no dish that can't be improved by the addition of a poached egg. Thus the need to address the following:

HOW TO MAKE PERFECT POACHED EGGS

When you crack an egg into hot water, much of the loose white separates from the thick white, leaving something resembling a rumpled bed sheet with a yolk attached in a haze of confetti water. Countless people advise adding vinegar to the poaching water to help prevent flyaway whites, as acid can help speed coagulation. Do not do this! I repeat, do *not* add vinegar to the water in which you're poaching eggs. It does nothing more than force you to rinse off your sour egg. The trick, as I read in Harold McGee's invaluable book *On Food and Cooking*, is to let the runny whites drain off by putting the egg in a slotted spoon before placing it in water (it

works so well that I created my Badass Perforated Egg Spoon, a slotted spoon with an extra-deep bowl, just for this purpose—see the "Shop" page at ruhlman.com). This technique gives you a gorgeously smooth, oval poached egg without all those scraggly whites adhering to it. Simply crack an egg into a ramekin, pour it from the ramekin through a deep perforated spoon into another ramekin, then return it to the first ramekin and it's ready to go.

So, to poach an egg perfectly: Bring a pot of water to a simmer, then reduce the flame to low or remove the pot from the burner completely. Give the water a stir to keep the egg from sticking to the bottom (the stirring also helps make the eggs more shapely), and drop your drained egg into the gently swirling water. When the white has completely congealed, after about 90 seconds, use your perforated spoon to lift the egg out of the water, swooshing the water underneath the egg if necessary to help you lift it (if you see that the egg isn't quite done, just return it to the water until it is). Allow any excess water to drain off; you may need to tilt the egg so that any water collecting on the white can run off, or touch a paper towel to its surface. Serve immediately.

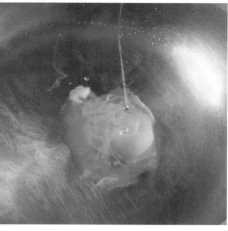

I. / Strain the raw egg, allowing the loose white to drain off.

2. / Add the egg to water that has simmered, first stirring the water to prevent the white from sticking.

3. / Notice how few flyaway whites there are in the water.

4. / Gently lift the poached egg out of the water.

5. / Check to make sure the egg is done to your liking and allow it to drain on a paper towel.

6. / A poached egg can be served on virtually any dish and improve it—a salad, a sandwich, a hamburger. Here I put it on warm shaved ham and toast, before adding hollandaise (next page).

Eggs Benedict

SERVES 4

There is simply no reason this restaurant/hotel buffet-line brunch favorite shouldn't be served more often at home. No matter how you prepare it, this is one of the most luxurious and wonderful dishes I know of. I love that the sauce is made of yolk and butter—that lovely egg-butter pairing doubled, egg and butter on top of another egg ("Waiter, I'd like an egg, with butter and more egg on top, please").

I grew up expecting the ham to be in the form of Canadian bacon, which is cured and smoked pork loin, and it's likely that became standard because the circumference of the pork loin matches the English muffin. That's why I include it here, but you can use any kind of ham or cured pork, such as prosciutto or bacon, or even pulled pork or duck confit—just don't call it eggs Benedict, which is English muffin, Canadian bacon, poached egg, and hollandaise sauce. I recommend Bays brand English muffins, which can be found in the refrigerated section of most supermarkets. I prefer the larger, crustier bottom half and simply serve the top half alongside each plate; or you can toast just two English muffins and serve half to each person.

4 English muffins, halved

4 (¼-inch/1-centimeter) slices Canadian bacon

4 eggs

1 cup/240 milliliters hollandaise sauce (either traditional or blender version, page 168)

Salt and pepper to taste

1 tablespoon chopped fresh chives or parsley (optional)

Toast the English muffin bottoms. If using a toaster oven, put the Canadian bacon on the English muffins and keep toasting to heat the bacon. If using a pop-up toaster, heat the Canadian bacon gently in a microwave—or, better yet, sauté in butter! Then toast the English muffin tops.

Meanwhile, bring a large pot of water to a boil and prepare the eggs by draining off the whites as described on page 44. When ready to serve, drop the eggs into the water and remove the pot from the heat. Put an English muffin bottom on each of four plates and a piece of Canadian bacon atop each muffin. When the eggs are cooked (after about 90 seconds), remove them from the water, allow them to drain, and place one atop each Canadian bacon–topped muffin. Spoon the hollandaise over the eggs, garnish with chives, if desired, and serve immediately, with the English muffin tops alongside.

Poached Duck Egg
on Duck Confit Hash

SERVES 4

*A friend of a friend connected me with some farmers
who raise ducks, and they often find themselves with
more duck eggs on their hands than they can eat. I am
the happy recipient of them and urge you to seek out
duck eggs at your local farmers' market if possible.
Some Whole Foods Markets also sell duck eggs. While
all bird eggs taste more or less the same, duck eggs are
larger than chicken eggs and a little more oblong, with
very large yolks and considerably less white relative to
the yolk, thus richer.*

*I love to make a duck-egg omelet (filled with duck
confit and mushrooms), scrambled duck egg on toast,
or, my favorite, poached duck egg nestled on a hash
of rich duck confit, potatoes, and onions. I confit duck
legs in olive oil to keep on hand all winter long (see
my site, ruhlman.com, for how to make this). Or you
can prepare the duck legs specifically for this dish by
cooking them in a covered baking dish with a sliced
onion at 325°F/165°C for 90 minutes.*

¼ cup/60 milliliters duck fat, confit fat,
or vegetable oil

2 russet potatoes, peeled and cut into small
dice (about 1½ pounds/680 grams)

Salt and freshly ground black pepper

1 medium onion, cut into small dice

4 confit or braised duck legs, bones discarded,
skin and meat coarsely chopped

2 tablespoons Dijon mustard

4 duck eggs

1 teaspoon minced garlic (optional)

1 tablespoon minced fresh parsley (optional)

Heat the fat in a large skillet over high heat. Add
the potato, tossing to coat it with the fat. Reduce
the heat to medium-high and cook till the potatoes
begin to turn brown, about 20 minutes. Season
to taste with salt and pepper. Add the onion and
chopped duck meat and skin and continue cooking
until the onion begins to brown, another 10 minutes
or so (the cooking time will be determined by how
small you've cut the onion). Stir in the mustard and
reduce the heat to low.

When the hash is done, bring the poaching water
to a boil and poach the duck eggs (see page 44; the
same procedure applies for duck eggs). Stir the
garlic and parsley into the hash, if desired, and
divide the hash among four plates. Rest a duck egg
in the center of the hash. Season the egg with salt
and pepper and serve.

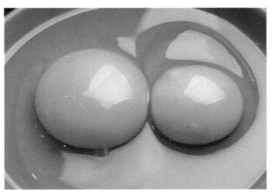

*A duck egg (left) has a considerably larger yolk than
a hen egg (right).*

Poached in Sauce

WATER IS A FABULOUS MEDIUM FOR POACH-ing eggs, but it's not the only fluid that works. Eggs can be poached in anything that's bubbling on your stove, whether soup, stew, or sauce.

When poaching in something you're going to eat, draining off the loose egg white is even more important; you don't want it messing up a nice sauce or broth (unless of course you're making egg drop soup, page 69). See page 44 for how to strain an egg before poaching.

The best-known version of eggs in broth is the Italian *uova in brodetto,* the *brodetto* being the diminutive form of *brodo,* "broth." In America you often see this in the form of eggs in tomato sauce, known as eggs in purgatory, and usually served on toast. In Israeli cuisine it's called *shakshuka,* and no doubt eggs poached in tomato sauce has a place in many cuisines because, well, it's so damned good. I like to spice it up, puttanesca style, with garlic, red pepper flakes, olives, and capers, but if you want a last-minute dish or a quick breakfast, a good jarred tomato sauce works fine, because the egg makes everything better. (If you have time, sauté a little chopped onion before adding the jarred sauce; this improves the flavor well beyond the effort required.)

The proper French version of eggs poached in broth calls for a reduction sauce of half wine and half veal or beef stock. I really think it ought to be made with homemade stock, because boxed stock isn't very good, and when you reduce something not very good, the not very good part gets intensified. This stock-wine reduction is quickly thickened with *beurre manié* (butter with flour kneaded into it) after the eggs are poached in it, then served over the egg.

Oeufs en Meurette
(Eggs Poached in Red Wine Sauce)

SERVES 4

This is a French classic from Burgundy, eggs poached in red wine and stock, which then becomes the sauce for the eggs. There are a number of ways to do this. At a restaurant the eggs would be poached in the wine and chilled in an ice bath while the rest of the components are prepared; the sauce would be reduced and thickened, then reheated for service. For this home version, I do the reduction first, then cook the eggs, then thicken the sauce.

Whenever you cook with wine, use a wine you would happily drink, but not a special-occasion wine. A ten-dollar bottle will do, and what you don't use in the sauce, you can drink with the eggs.

Veal stock is a great ingredient to have in the kitchen and really makes this dish the best it can be (there's a recipe for it on my site, ruhlman.com), but you can use a rich homemade chicken stock with good results. These eggs are best served on toast, a piece of baguette, or the bottom half of an English muffin—something with crunch that will also soak up the sauce. Choose your own side components—bacon or lardons are popular, of course, and would be my choice. Be sure to have them all ready before you poach the eggs.

1 shallot, finely diced

4 tablespoons/60 grams butter, at room temperature

½ teaspoon salt

2 teaspoons tomato paste

2 cups/480 milliliters dry red wine

2 cups/480 milliliters brown veal stock
or homemade roasted chicken stock

2 teaspoons sugar

1 bay leaf

Freshly ground black pepper

3 tablespoons flour

4 slices bread

4 eggs

1 tablespoon minced fresh parsley

Combine the shallot and 1 tablespoon/15 grams of the butter in a medium saucepan over medium heat. When the butter is melted, add the salt. Cook, stirring, until the shallot is translucent. Add the tomato paste and cook for 30 seconds. Add the wine, stock, sugar, bay leaf, and a few grindings of pepper and simmer until the liquid has reduced by a little more than half, 5 to 10 minutes.

While it's reducing, in a small bowl combine the remaining 3 tablespoons/45 grams butter with the flour and mash and knead it with a spoon till the flour is completely mixed into the butter. Cover and refrigerate this *beurre manié*. Toast the bread and place one slice on each of four plates.

Crack the eggs into individual ramekins and strain them to get rid of any loose egg white (see page 44). When the wine and stock have reduced, add the eggs and cook them gently in the sauce. Spoon the sauce over the tops of the eggs if they're poking up through the sauce. When the whites are completely set (after about 90 seconds, but always judge by sight), remove each egg and place it on a slice of toasted bread.

Strain the reduced sauce into a clean pan over high heat and bring to a simmer, then reduce the heat to medium-high. Whisk in the *beurre manié* to thicken the sauce. Spoon the sauce over the eggs and toasted bread and garnish with the parsley. Serve immediately with bacon or other sides.

Eggs in Puttanesca Sauce with Angel Hair Pasta

SERVES 4

Pasta puttanesca translates as whore's pasta, allegedly because it was hastily thrown together by Sicilian hookers between clients. But what it always designates is a spicy tomato sauce with lots of salty, umami-giving ingredients. It usually includes anchovies, but I'm using fish sauce here because it's one of my invaluable pantry items, always on hand. Add red pepper flakes, kalamata olives, capers, and eggs to make a fabulous pasta dish—and you'll have some sauce left over for other uses. This dish is usually served on a thick piece of crusty toasted bread, but here I'm pairing it with pasta instead.

You can puree canned tomatoes in a blender, or just stick an immersion blender right in the can, but you should first pour off some of the tomato juice into the pan with the onions or you'll have a mess—trust me.

1 Spanish onion, cut into small dice

4 garlic cloves, smashed with the flat side of a knife and roughly chopped

1 tablespoon extra-virgin olive oil

1 teaspoon salt, plus more to taste

1 teaspoon red pepper flakes

1 cup/240 milliliters dry red wine

1 (28-ounce/794-gram) can whole peeled tomatoes, pureed, or 10 fresh Roma tomatoes, broiled for 15 minutes and pureed

1 bay leaf or 2 teaspoons dried oregano (or both)

½ tablespoon fish sauce or 4 anchovies, roughly chopped

½ cup/90 grams pitted, chopped kalamata olives

2 tablespoons capers

4 eggs

1 pound/450 grams angel hair pasta or thin spaghetti, cooked al dente and tossed with extra-virgin olive oil or butter, kept warm in a covered pot

In a large sauté pan or skillet over medium-high heat, sauté the onion and garlic in the olive oil, adding the salt as you do. Stir until the onion and garlic are tender and translucent, then add the red pepper flakes and stir to cook them and coat them with the oil.

Add the wine and bring it to a simmer. Add the pureed tomatoes, the bay leaf and/or oregano, and bring it back to a simmer. Reduce the heat to low and cook the sauce till it's nice and thick, about 1 hour. The sauce can be prepared in advance up to this point, allowed to cool, and stored in a covered container in the refrigerator for up to 3 days.

Remove and discard the bay leaf and add the fish sauce (or anchovies), olives, and capers. If the sauce was refrigerated, bring it to a full simmer over medium heat, then turn the heat to low. Lower each egg into the sauce with a ladle, making a small well in the sauce with the ladle to contain it. Cover the pan and cook the eggs until the whites are set, 3 to 6 minutes.

Divide the warm pasta among four serving dishes. Spoon the sauce over the pasta, topping each portion with an egg and finishing each dish with more sauce as needed. Serve immediately.

I. / Use a ladle to put the eggs into the sauce, pressing the bowl of the ladle down into the sauce to create a divot that will contain them.

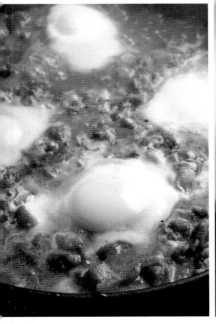

2. / Cook covered just until the whites are set, checking frequently to avoid overcooking.

3. / Top the pasta with sauce, followed by an egg.

Poached in a Bag

THIS IS THE SECOND OF TWO EGG TECH-niques I picked up on Twitter. Why would you want to poach an egg in a plastic bag? Because you can. Because it keeps a compact shape. Because you capture the whole egg and don't lose the loose part of the egg. And because you can flavor the egg with oil (it's important to oil the bag first so that the egg doesn't stick to it). You might also do it to serve numerous poached eggs at once; pop them straight into an ice bath and reheat as needed. (If you're concerned about chemicals from the plastic getting into the food, use Glad plastic bags, which don't contain BPAs or phthalates.)

Poached-in-a-Bag Egg Sandwich with Caramelized Onion and Roasted Red Pepper

SERVES 4

This is simply an excuse to have an egg sandwich. The caramelized onion and roasted red pepper make it especially delicious. Or create your own variation: bacon, Parmigiano-Reggiano, and parsley (alla carbonara); butter and sautéed spinach (Florentine); truffle butter and mushrooms. Or you could just spread some mayo on the muffin and be done with it. Serving it on an English muffin is not just a tasty way to go, it's also practical: the holey crumb helps catch the yolk when you bite into it. But you definitely want to eat this over a plate; use the muffin to soak up any fallen yolk.

4 teaspoons extra-virgin olive oil

4 eggs

1 teaspoon butter, plus more for the English muffins

½ onion, thinly sliced

1 red bell pepper, charred black over a flame or under a broiler, then peeled and diced

Salt and freshly ground black pepper

¼ teaspoon red or white wine vinegar

4 English muffins

Butter

If you wish to cook your eggs ahead of time, bring a medium pot of water to a simmer over high heat, then reduce the heat so that water is gently simmering; prepare an ice bath (half ice, half water). Put 1 teaspoon olive oil into each of four small plastic bags, then crack an egg into each bag. Twist each bag closed and secure it with a twist tie. Lower the bags into the simmering water and cook for 4 minutes. Transfer the bags to the ice bath and put the whole thing in the refrigerator until you're ready to serve. At that point, return the bags to simmering water for 90 seconds to reheat before serving.

When you're ready to prepare the sandwiches, heat the butter over medium heat and sauté the onion gently till nicely browned and caramelized, 15 to 20 minutes. Add the red bell pepper to reheat, season to taste with salt and pepper, and then add the vinegar.

Toast and butter the English muffins.

If you haven't made the eggs ahead of time, cook them now as described above. Divide the onion-pepper mixture among the four muffin bottoms. Place a cooked egg on each—they will slip easily out of their oiled bags. Season the eggs with salt and pepper and top with the muffin tops. Serve immediately.

Part Three

Egg / Whole / Cooked out of Shell

Blended

This branch of the egg cookery flowchart features recipes using the whole egg, out of its shell, and blended. The egg becomes a different entity altogether when the fatty, rich yolk is interspersed with the lean and powerful proteins of the white. A beautiful entity. Like all beautiful things, though, the blended egg can be used carelessly (when it's not fully mixed, for instance) or even badly abused, as scrambled eggs all too often are. But the blended egg can also be transformed into some of the most ethereal creations on earth.

When the yolk and white join forces, the egg becomes a dynamo, a powerhouse ingredient. The blended egg is a remarkable tool when it's whipped to a froth, leavening cakes and quick breads. When combined with liquids and cooked gently, it creates textural heaven in the form of custard. It helps to bind bread crumbs to the floured surfaces of meat and gives a glossy golden hue to breads and crusts when it's brushed on the still-baking goods. And it is an enriching ingredient in a whole continuum of flour-based food, from bread to pasta, cookies to crêpes.

• • •

Fried (Dry Heat)

HOW TO MAKE PERFECT SCRAMBLED EGGS

SCRAMBLED EGGS—A NO-BRAINER, RIGHT? Only if you think first. This is probably the most badly abused technique in the entire repertoire of the egg, and as scrambled is one of the most common forms of cooked eggs, the abuse is especially unfortunate. They are abused by being overcooked, way overcooked, cooked dry. The key to perfect scrambled eggs is gentle heat. In an earlier book, *Ruhlman's Twenty*, I recommended scrambling eggs in what amounts to a double boiler, so that the eggs never go above 212°F/100°C. You can overcook them in a double boiler, but the cooking happens much more slowly, so you have much more control. Once you know how to properly scramble eggs, or rather what properly scrambled eggs taste like—light, silky, the delicate curds essentially sauced by warm but uncongealed egg—you can then move, if you feel comfortable doing so, to a pan over direct heat. You'll need to use very low heat and to pay careful attention the entire time, moderating the heat by lifting the pan above the burner to ensure you don't cook the eggs too quickly or too much.

The best way to learn how to properly scramble eggs yourself—eggs that make people swoon; that make people think to themselves, "These are the best scrambled eggs I've ever had!"; that make people exclaim, "I never knew scrambled eggs could be so amazing!"—is to cook them in a saucier or other round pan or in a double-boiler insert over simmering water. I use a stainless-steel saucier pan that floats in a pot of simmering water. If you have a nonstick pan, that's best, because egg will stick to most surfaces at this temperature and the pan will be a pain to scrub clean.

Thoroughly blend your eggs, two per person.

By thoroughly blended I mean *absolute uniformity*. Use a whisk, a handheld immersion blender, or a countertop blender and blend well. You don't want them too frothy—you're not making a cake—but you don't want to be able to spot any white not mixed fully into the yellow. If you're using an electric appliance to mix the eggs, the bubbles and froth will go away as you cook the eggs.

You can give them a pinch of salt at this point if you wish so that it dissolves, or wait to the end if you want the salt flavor to be more distinctive.

And that's it for preparation: a pot of water simmering on the stove, a metal cooking vessel (you can use a Pyrex bowl, but heat transfer will be very slow), and eggs blended to uniformity. If you want additional flavors—seasonings such as cayenne or black pepper or curry; fats such as goat or cheddar cheese, truffle butter, olive oil; aromatic or tasty herbs or vegetables such as chives, tarragon, shallot, mushroom—have these ready, but these scrambled eggs you're about to make will be fabulous with just the eggs cooked in some butter, with salt and toast. I like to pare down to essentials, get those essentials right, and then build from there.

Float your cooking vessel in the simmering water and get your bread toasting; give the eggs a multiple-finger pinch of salt and another few whisks or a pulse of the blender. Put a couple teaspoons of butter into the floating pan as it starts to get hot from the simmering water below. When it's melted, pour in the eggs and, using a rubber spatula, begin to cook the eggs. Stir plenty and gently in the beginning as the cool eggs and the hot pan adjust to one another, 30 seconds or so. Then stir incrementally, allowing the first curds to form. Lift and fold them into the fluid egg. Now is when you might want to add cheese or sautéed mushrooms or shallot (other flavors such as fresh herbs or truffle might go later), but for now let's focus on the eggs, curdling in the pan.

Continue to fold and stir, and as you see steam rising and the whole mixture is beginning to get hot, pay close attention. Ask someone to butter the toast and to make sure the coffee is hot and ready or the Champagne is uncorked.

Continuously, more or less, stir and fold the eggs until about two-thirds of the eggs are stiff and one-third is viscous but fluid. Remove the pan from the water and continue to stir until the curds appear to be sauced by the fluid part of the eggs. Now they are ready to be served. Remember that just because you took the pan out of the water doesn't mean the eggs have stopped cooking— they're still cooking in the residual heat of the pan. So hie them hence to warm plates with buttered toast. Finish with chives, a pat of butter, *fleur de sel*, freshly ground pepper, whatever, but be sure to do this: rejoice at the perfect scrambled eggs you've just prepared. Once you've experienced delicate egg curds lightly sauced by their more fluid self, replicate the effect using direct heat, preferably a nonstick pan on a low flame or burner, lifting the pan above the flame or burner as needed to regulate the heat. Your life will be immeasurably better.

Now begin to experiment with flavors. Use flavors that go well with eggs: mushroom, onion and its brethren (chives, scallion, shallot), or freshly shaved white truffle (I wish!). Donna loves to throw diced or shredded cheese in there, anything from mild mozzarella to acidic goat cheese, rich cheddar or smoked Gouda. I know of no cheese that doesn't work, but the better the cheese, the better the eggs. All of that is up to your taste now that you've perfected the scrambled egg.

Scrambled Eggs with Fines Herbes

SERVES 4

My favorite fresh herb mixture is fines herbes, *equal parts parsley, tarragon, chervil, and chives. I grow all of these soft, fragrant, volatile herbs, but the chervil doesn't survive long into the summer. Chervil has a lovely shape and a delicate tarragon flavor, so if I'm out, I use more tarragon—indeed, you might want to use only tarragon. But I like the combination of the tarragon and chervil with the oniony chive and floral flat-leaf parsley for its complexity and aroma when it lands on the hot eggs (you'd lose the freshness if you cooked them with the eggs; though if you want, you can stir half of the herbs into the eggs just before serving). I highly recommend serving this in the late morning with excellent buttered toast and a glass of Champagne.*

1 tablespoon butter

4 eggs, whipped to a uniform pale yellow

¼ to ½ teaspoon salt

1 teaspoon *each* minced fresh flat-leaf parsley, tarragon, chervil, and chives, combined

Bring a large pot of water to a simmer over medium-high heat. Meanwhile, ready everything you intend to serve with the eggs (toast, coffee, steamed asparagus, Champagne, up to you).

When the water is simmering, float a high-sided pan in the water and add the butter to the pan. When the pan is hot and the butter melted, add the eggs and the salt and stir more or less continuously until they are perfectly cooked (see the instructions starting on page 59).

Divide the eggs among four plates. Sprinkle 1 teaspoon of the *fines herbes* mixture over each portion and serve immediately. (Though they're good chilled, scrambled eggs are better eaten hot rather than lukewarm.)

The Omelet

THE WORD *OMELET* ORIGINALLY DERIVES from the Latin for "little plate," and omelets are usually made individually. You quickly cook one or two eggs while stirring rapidly and continuously to make the curds very fine, then stop the stirring to let the eggs set in the pan. When the omelet is just barely cooked, you grip the handle of the pan, palm up, and roll the egg from the handle side of the pan out of the pan and over the opposite edge in, one hopes, a lovely long oval of delicately pale, perfectly smooth, uniformly yellow egg. It takes practice—mistakes are delicious and successes are high-five-worthy.

The omelet becomes more visually appealing if you put some soft butter on top to give it a glossy shine and, if you wish, some minced chives, but really, an omelet is simply an elegant, shapely form of the scrambled egg.

We've come to think of omelets in America as always being stuffed with something—mushrooms and bell peppers and ham and cheese—so that there's more stuffing than egg. People debate whether to add cream or water or even olive oil, and you can, but why? Instead, it's worth pausing to appreciate the simple beauty of the omelet. All egg, enriched with a little butter and nothing more. If you have access to very fresh eggs from a friend or farmer near you and some delicious butter, an omelet with a glass of wine and maybe some charcuterie makes an excellent light meal. Go read Elizabeth David's *An Omelette and a Glass of Wine* if you don't believe me.

Before we developed really good nonstick pans, cooks relied on creating a nonstick surface on their steel pans and reserved them only for omelets, allowing no soap anywhere near them. But I highly recommend that home cooks use a good, lovingly cared for nonstick pan for omelet making. They really do take the risk of sticking out of the equation, not to mention the omelet-pan fanaticism you'll find among traditional chefs.

Because of the omelet's simplicity, errors are glaring. Many restaurant chefs will ask an applicant to make an omelet, because omelet technique tells a chef many things about the finesse and skills of a young cook.

HOW TO MAKE A PERFECT OMELET

Again, I'd like to reiterate that everyone should first make a plain omelet—two eggs, a pat of butter, a pinch of salt—to appreciate what an omelet is. I often add cheese or mushrooms to make the omelet more interesting and fun to eat. But it's important to first understand the foundation those garnishes are enhancing.

To make an omelet, crack the eggs into a bowl and whisk or blend till they are uniformly combined and no clear white remains floating on the surface. Give it a three-finger pinch of salt and stir in the salt.

Put a nonstick pan over medium heat and let the pan get hot, a couple minutes or so, depending on your stovetop. Have a heatproof rubber spatula ready, and warm a plate in the microwave. Add a pat of butter (about 1 tablespoon) to the pan. It should melt and bubble immediately but not brown. After the butter has melted and coats the bottom of the pan, pour in the eggs.

Shake the pan back and forth while stirring the eggs with the spatula. Stirring continuously will give you a finely textured curd. After about 30 seconds of stirring, stop and let the omelet continue cooking until there remains the thinnest liquid film on top, another 60 seconds or so. Remove it from the heat and allow it to finish cooking just sitting there in the pan (after all, you're not a line cook getting thirty-nine orders at once). With the pan handle at three o'clock, and your warm plate at nine o'clock (reverse this if you're a lefty), grip the handle from underneath and tilt the pan toward the plate. Using the spatula, encourage the front end of the omelet to slide out (you may need to give the pan a rap on a cutting board to loosen the egg, then nudge it from underneath to get it sliding) and roll the omelet over itself and onto a plate. The heat from the pan should finish cooking the omelet; it should be moist but you shouldn't have sauce on your plate. If it's not perfectly shaped, use your hands (which you've been washing continually, what with being in the kitchen, cracking eggs, etc.) to make it pretty and uniform. It's fairly pliable at this point, so you can tuck freely if needed. Run a little soft butter over the top so that it melts and gives the omelet a nice shine. Finish with some *fleur de sel* or Maldon salt if you have it, and some chives always look nice.

Eat this immediately.

1. / When the pan is hot and the butter is melted, your pan is ready for the eggs.

2. / Swirling both the pan and the spatula, mix the eggs in the pan to create a very fine curd on the bottom while heating the eggs throughout.

4. / Roll and slide the omelet onto a plate. Remember that you will be able to shape it after it's out of the pan.

3. / Stop stirring and allow the eggs to set. When the omelet has a very thin film of loose egg on top, it's ready to be plated.

5. / Notice the pale uniform color of the omelet, with no browning.

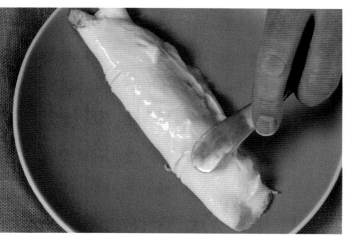

6. / Shape the omelet as you wish and finish with a pat of butter.

Omelet with Creamy Morel Mushrooms

SERVES 2

An omelet composed solely of egg and brushed with butter is great on its own, but to cut into an omelet and see gooey cheese run out is a pleasure. Omelets do make a lovely package for sautéed mushrooms. So that's what I'm offering here, a creamy mixture of morel mushrooms encased in delicately set egg. Of course any kind of mushroom will work—button mushrooms, shiitakes, or other wild mushrooms (though I like to sear buttons and portobellos to give them color and flavor). It makes the cook's work easier if the filling is very hot, so that it will contribute to the cooking of the center of the omelet when added.

If you live where morels grow and can harvest your own or have a source for good fresh morels, lucky you! I don't, but morels dry very well, and several online sources sell them (our fresh morels came from a wonderful Michigan company called Earthy Delights). Dried morels should be reconstituted according to the instructions on the package, then halved and used as instructed here. Morels come up when ramps do, so if this is an option, use them instead of the shallot; thinly slice the whites of the ramps and sauté them with the mushrooms, then mince the greens and add them to the sauce at the last minute.

2 tablespoons butter, plus more for serving

1 tablespoon minced shallot (or 6 ramps, prepared as described above)

Salt

16 fresh morels, halved, or ½ ounce/15 grams dried morels, reconstituted in water

Freshly ground black pepper

½ cup/120 milliliters heavy cream

4 eggs, thoroughly blended

1 teaspoon minced fresh chives (optional)

Melt 1 tablespoon of the butter in a small sauté pan over medium heat and add the shallot (or whites of ramps) and a healthy pinch of salt (¼ teaspoon if you must measure). Cook the shallots in the butter till they're tender. Add the morels and stir to heat and coat with butter. Grind some pepper over the mushrooms. Add the cream and bring to a simmer, then reduce the heat and cook until the cream has thickened and coats the morels. (Cream will break if you overcook it, so don't.) Remove the pan from the heat.

In a medium sauté pan, melt the remaining 1 tablespoon butter over medium heat. Add the eggs and cook the omelet as instructed on pages 61–62. When the omelet is set, and there is a thin film of liquidy egg on top, scatter the hot mushrooms down the center of the omelet. Roll the omelet out of the pan and onto a warm plate. Slide a little butter over the top if you wish, garnish with chives if desired, and add more salt and pepper to taste. Cut the omelet in half crosswise and transfer one half to another warm plate. Serve immediately.

Two equally fine ways to serve an omelet: with the garnish rolled up inside (top and bottom left) or spooned over the top (right).

1. / *The frittata is one of the easiest egg preparations. Simply pour the eggs over the cooked ingredients—here, potato and onion—and let them cook.*

2. / *Cheese makes egg and potato even better.*

3. / *Run a spatula around the edge to loosen the frittata. Either invert it onto a plate and slide it back into the pan or, my preference, place the pan beneath the broiler until the egg is set and then invert onto a cutting board.*

4. / *Garnish as you wish, with herbs, avocado, or more cheese, then slice and serve.*

Potato, Onion, and Cheese Frittata

SERVES 4

This was the first dish I learned how to make on my own, when I was in the fifth grade. As the only child of working parents, I often made it as an after-school meal, to tide me over until they got home and we could eat a late dinner together. I still remember the little nonstick pan I cooked it in. In the beginning I simply used small-diced potatoes, cooked till they were soft. I poured in whisked eggs, fried the mixture over medium heat till it was almost set, inverted it onto a plate, and slipped it back into the pan to finish it. The top was mottled brown, the potatoes and eggs tender, and I'd eat it lying on the carpeting of our den watching Gilligan's Island. *It was simple, delicious, and nourishing.*

Now I make enough for the whole family, in a larger pan, so inverting is more difficult. You can cover it to set the top, invert it onto a plate, and slide it back into the pan; but it's easiest to finish it beneath a broiler just until the eggs are set. However you finish it, invert it onto a cutting board or plate before serving so that you present the mottled brown bottom surface.

A frittata is simply an Italian omelet, and you can use any additional ingredients you wish. I'm making this a little more complex than my fifth-grade version, adding onion to the browned potato and cheddar cheese to the egg. When I tested this recipe, I gave a slice to my son, James, who was cutting up an avocado. We put some avocado on top and it was fabulous. The frittata is infinitely variable.

1 small potato, peeled and cut into small dice (about 1 cup/225 grams)

2 tablespoons extra-virgin olive oil

Salt

½ onion, cut into small dice (about ½ cup/100 grams)

6 eggs, thoroughly blended

½ cup/60 grams shredded cheddar cheese

Freshly ground black pepper

2 avocados, peeled, pitted, and diced (optional)

Preheat the broiler.

In a medium nonstick fry pan, combine the potatoes and olive oil over medium-high heat and stir or toss them in the pan to coat the potatoes with oil. Add a three-finger pinch of salt, just to coat the surface. When the potatoes are lightly browned, add the onions, salt to coat the onions, and continue to cook until the onions are tender, stirring or tossing the potato and onion.

Place the eggs in a medium bowl and add the cheese, along with ½ teaspoon salt and several grinds of pepper, and stir to combine and disperse the cheese. Pour the egg mixture over the potatoes and onions and reduce the heat to medium, swirling the pan so that the eggs even out. Cook until the edges are set, a couple of minutes depending on the heat level, checking to make sure that the eggs aren't sticking. Place the pan underneath the broiler until the eggs are just set, a minute or two depending on your broiler. When the top is set, invert the frittata onto a cutting board, cover with the diced avocado, if using, and cut into wedges. Serve.

Poached (Wet Heat)

Daniel Patterson's Poached Omelet

SERVES 1

Eggs are so versatile, and so inexpensive, they're fun to experiment with. (I put some in the hot ashes of our fireplace, a technique from the Middle Ages; they were brown, overcooked, and sulfuric—but worth a try!)

The talented Daniel Patterson, chef-owner of the restaurant Coi in San Francisco, wrote in the New York Times *about an egg experiment he did that seems so obvious I'm amazed it's not simply common practice. It's been widely written about since the January 2006 article appeared; given the power of social media regarding food information, word spread rapidly.*

"Then one day," Patterson writes, tired of eating the same old scrambled eggs, "I had an idea for a new way to cook eggs—probably not new to the world, but new to me. It was a little humbling. After more than 20 years of cooking in restaurants, I had clearly failed to master basic egg cookery. I took a moment to ponder this, but then my curiosity got the better of me: what would happen, I wondered, if I beat the eggs before putting them in the water? I expected that they would act much as the intact eggs did and bind quickly, but I did not expect them to set into the lightest, most delicate scrambled eggs imaginable. I became so excited that I immediately reverted to my old ways, eating them standing up in the kitchen."

The technique is probably the easiest and most foolproof method devised for cooking eggs to such delicate consistency. Simply give boiling water a swirl, pour the blended egg into it, and strain after 10 or 20 seconds. (Patterson and others, including myself, recommend first straining off the loose white, which you should definitely do for whole poached eggs, as well—see page 44.) Blended poached eggs are incomparably fluffy and light—the main pleasure

here in fact is their ethereal texture—so I think a flavorful garnish is important. I love these with some good olive oil and truffle salt, or olive oil and Parmigiano-Reggiano. But salt and pepper and some fresh herbs are fine, too. Marlene Newell, my chief recipe tester, longed to toast an English muffin with some cheddar and top it with the eggs.

While most of the water is expelled, they'll usually trap some water, so do your best to strain off as much water as possible. I tried different methods but couldn't improve on Patterson's, so this is taken straight from him. It's brilliant.

Salt

2 eggs, strained of the loose white and blended to uniformity

1 tablespoon extra-virgin olive oil

Several gratings of Parmigiano-Reggiano

Bring a 2-quart pot of pleasantly salted water (a teaspoon or two) to a low boil. Give the water a swirl with a spoon to create enough current to keep the egg whites from sinking to the bottom and sticking there. Pour in the eggs. After the eggs have risen to the surface and are cooked, 20 to 30 seconds, hold back the eggs with a spoon and pour off as much water as possible, then dump the eggs into a strainer to get rid of any remaining water. Serve the eggs in a bowl, with the olive oil and grated Parmigiano and more salt if needed.

Traditional Egg Flower Soup

SERVES 4

Here blended eggs are poached in a delicious stock and streamed into the hot liquid, rather than dumped in as with Chef Patterson's poached eggs. I include this recipe because it is so delicious, simple, and nourishing. But it's paramount that you use a chicken stock that is delicious on its own (meaning you've made it yourself, stolen it from a friend or family member who has made it, or bought it frozen from a very good source). Egg can be swirled into any delicious broth and served as a soup, but here I'd like to offer a traditional egg "drop" soup in the Chinese fashion, a dish that ought to be more common around the world.

As Eileen Yin-Fei Lo notes in her fine book The Chinese Kitchen, *egg drop soup in America has become dull, unnecessarily thickened with cornstarch, and often made with badly cooked, lumpy eggs. "In China, this soup,* don far tong,*" she writes, "translates as 'egg flower soup.'" How much more lovely is that than "drop"? Our name is the literary equivalent of our actual debasing. So here it is, back to the Chinese, with fresh delicious stock, eggs, and scallion for garnish. Make as much or as little as you wish, planning on 1 egg per 1 cup broth per person. The key to getting the right texture of the eggs, the flowerlike delicacy, is in the gentle heat of the liquid and gentle whisking.*

1 quart/1 liter delicious chicken broth

Salt

2 teaspoons fish sauce (optional)

4 eggs, beaten

2 scallions, sliced feather-thin on a bias, including the white and some green

Freshly ground black pepper

Bring the broth to a simmer in a large saucepan over medium heat. Taste it. Add salt, stir it, and taste again. When it is nicely seasoned, add the fish sauce, if using, and bring the soup to a boil. Turn the heat immediately to low (or remove it from the heat altogether if you're using an electric burner).

Give the broth a vigorous circular stirring with a large fork, then pour the eggs in a stream into the broth, whisking gently as you do to make a flower of the eggs.

Ladle into bowls and garnish each serving with scallions and freshly ground pepper. Serve.

NOTE: *For a more powerfully flavored soup, sauté scallion, minced ginger, and garlic in a little oil. Add the stock and cook gently—scarcely a bubble—for 20 minutes. Strain the infused stock into a clean pan and proceed with the above recipe.*

Egg / Whole / Cooked out of Shell / Blended

Baked (Dry Heat)

Marlene's Bacon and Sausage Breakfast Strata

SERVES 6 TO 8

I didn't even know what a strata was—a layered casserole in the annals of American cuisine—until my chief recipe tester, Marlene Newell, a Canadian, pleaded to include one. I said give me a killer strata and it's in. This one rocks. It's basically a bacon-sausage-onion bread pudding (or dressing—it would go great with a big roasted bird!). I like it as a hearty breakfast when you have lots of mouths to feed. It's a go-to for weekend brunch when guests are in town, because it can be made the night before with the leftover bread from dinner, and can sit in the fridge all night soaking up the custardy goodness, then baked in the morning straight from the fridge while someone mixes the Bloodies.

Like a quiche, it's excellent cold as well, and it reheats beautifully, so it could be made a day or two in advance and reheated as needed.

8 ounces/240 grams sliced bacon

8 ounces/240 grams bulk breakfast sausage

½ Spanish onion, cut into medium dice

6 eggs

1 cup/240 milliliters milk

1 cup/240 milliliters heavy cream

1 teaspoon mustard powder

1 teaspoon salt

1 teaspoon freshly ground black pepper

¼ teaspoon cayenne pepper

7 to 9 slices day-old French or Italian bread, cut into ½-inch slices or cubes, toasted or allowed to sit out for a day or two (enough for two layers in your dish)

3 cups/300 grams grated hard cheese (such as cheddar, Gruyère, or Emmentaler)

Preheat the oven to 325°F/165°C. Butter a 9-by-13-inch/23-by-33-centimeter baking dish and set aside.

Place the bacon slices in a large skillet, cover them with water, and put the skillet over high heat. When the water has cooked off, reduce the heat to medium and cook the bacon until nicely browned and crisp. Remove to a plate lined with paper towels. Add the sausage to the bacon fat in the pan. Cook the sausage, breaking it up as it cooks. Meanwhile, chop the bacon coarsely. When the sausage is nearly cooked through, add the onion and continue to cook until the onion is tender, another 5 minutes or so. Use a slotted spoon to transfer the sausage-onion mixture to the plate with the bacon.

A strata is in effect a savory bread pudding. A custard is poured over bread and other tasty ingredients and then baked until the custard is set.

Combine the eggs, milk, cream, mustard powder, salt, pepper, and cayenne in a large bowl or glass measuring cup. Whisk or blend with a hand blender until the custard is uniform.

Put half of the bread cubes in an even layer in the prepared baking dish. Sprinkle half of the bacon-sausage-onion mixture evenly across the bread. Sprinkle half of the cheese evenly over this. Repeat the layers. Pour the custard over them. The dish

can be baked right away or covered and refrigerated for up to a day. Bake until the center is hot and the top is invitingly browned, 45 minutes to 1 hour.

Cut and serve hot. Alternatively, let it cool, then chill it in the refrigerator and eat it cold, or cut the chilled strata into serving-size pieces and reheat in a 350°F/180°C oven to serve.

Egg Wash

BLENDED EGG IS USEFUL IN MANY WAYS
when applied to the exterior of food. There are
numerous variations, including batter for onion
rings and tempura. (I will get to the latter, as I am
a great fan of deep-fried foods.)

But here I am discussing something widely
referred to as egg wash. Egg wash is nothing more
than blended egg (often with water or milk added
to thin it out). If you don't want a baked product to
look dry, adding some egg wash to the surface is
usually a good solution. Brushing beaten egg on
dough (see the eggy challah recipe, page 93) results
in an appealing shiny and browned surface. The
protein in the white becomes shiny when cooked;
the water in the eggs also promotes the gelatiniza-
tion of starch, which enhances the shininess. The
glucose in the egg browns. Water, milk, or cream
can be added to the wash to thin it out and to
contribute slightly to browning. Yolk-only washes
result in a more deeply browned finish, but they can
burn in high-heat baking. White-only washes result
in a lighter, glossy finish and are often used on
delicate pastries, such as tuiles.

Egg wash also creates a wet, tacky surface to
which dry things will stick. My parents used to love
chicken coated in crushed cornflakes (I couldn't
stand it). I prefer panko, which are coarse Japanese-
style bread crumbs that yield a very crispy crust.
But there's no reason any wheat, corn, or rice
products won't work.

Dry sticks to wet and wet sticks to dry. This is
the nature of things. So when you're breading food,
no matter what you're using, it's best to have a
completely dry surface that the egg wash can
adhere to. Flour is typical, but you could try fine
cornmeal or even, say, pulverized pretzels. One
thing I don't like to do with egg wash is to season it.
Sure, you could put rosemary or pepper in it, but I
prefer to apply dry seasonings to whatever it is I'm
coating. I could countenance adding a liquid
seasoning, such as sriracha or some other hot sauce.
That's up to you. Here we're doing what's referred
to in culinary school as "standard breading
procedure." Flour, followed by egg wash, followed
by bread crumbs.

Breaded Chicken Cutlets with Dijon and Thyme

SERVES 4

This recipe uses my least favorite cut of meat, which also happens to be the most popular cut of meat in the American home kitchen. It's not a bad cut, but it is so lean that it is easily overcooked and has almost no flavor—it's the skim milk of the meat world. America's laziness and pervasive fear of fat has made this its go-to cut of meat for all the wrong reasons.

This is the only way I use the boneless, skinless chicken breast, and it's a sure-fire way to make it delicious and fun to eat, with its crispy exterior and tender juicy interior. I pound the breasts between sheets of plastic wrap to make the thickest part tender and, importantly, to give them a more uniform thickness so that the thin, tapered end doesn't overcook.

With a barrier of crumbs attached to the exterior by the miraculous egg, the meat stays tender and juicy, and it is easy to cook perfectly every time. There are any number of ways to flour the meat and dredge it in bread crumbs. I put flour and any seasonings (here, plenty of pepper) in a plastic bag to coat the chicken Shake 'n Bake style. I slip them through the beaten egg in a broad bowl and use a 9-by-13-inch/23-by-33-centimeter baking dish for dredging in crumbs.

Chief recipe tester Marlene Newell wanted to liven up the breading by putting Dijon and fresh thyme leaves in the egg wash. I liked the idea of additional flavoring but feared that plenty of good Dijon would be left in the egg wash. I suggested she instead try applying the mustard and thyme directly to the meat before breading it. She did and it worked fabulously well.

This same method can be used for any tender cut of meat, such as a pork cutlet or chop, veal, or frying fish (flounder, hake, cod, orange roughy). And feel free to vary the seasoning used for the flour—you might try 1 tablespoon paprika, garlic salt, or onion powder, or 1 teaspoon cayenne pepper.

1 cup/140 grams flour

1 tablespoon freshly ground black pepper or seasoning of your choice (optional), plus more for seasoning the chicken

2 eggs, blended to uniformity in a broad bowl that will accommodate the chicken

1½ to 2 cups/162 to 220 grams panko

4 boneless, skinless chicken breasts (halves)

Salt

2 tablespoons Dijon mustard

1 tablespoon fresh thyme leaves

About ⅓ cup/75 milliliters vegetable oil, depending on the size of your pan

4 lemon wedges, for serving (optional)

First set up your breading *mise en place*. Put the flour in a plastic bag and add the pepper or other seasoning; shake to distribute throughout the flour. Next to this, set the bowl of egg wash. Next to this, set a plate or baking dish with 1 cup of the panko, with more at the ready as needed. Have also on your counter a wire rack on which to set the breaded chicken (a rack will allow the underside of the chicken to stay as dry as possible, but you could use a baking dish, plate, or sheet of parchment paper).

Put each chicken breast between two sheets of plastic wrap and pound with a meat mallet or sauté pan until the meat is more or less flat and uniform in thickness, concentrating mainly on thinning out the fat end.

Give each breast a liberal sprinkle of salt and some grinds of black pepper on each side. Spread the top of each breast with a couple of teaspoons Dijon, then sprinkle the thyme over each.

Gently put two breasts in the bag of flour and flip the bag or the breasts to dust the other side of the breasts. Remove them from the bag, shaking off any excess flour, and place them on the rack. Repeat with the remaining two breasts.

Slip one floured breast into the egg wash and remove it when it is evenly coated with egg, allowing any excess egg to fall back into the bowl. Press the breast into the panko. Shake the pan or plate back and forth with your dry hand to toss the crumbs onto the top of the breast, then flip the breast and press it firmly into the bread crumbs. Continue to flip and press it until it is uniformly coated with bread crumbs. Place it on the rack. Repeat with the remaining chicken breasts.

Pour about ¼ inch/6 millimeters oil into a sauté pan large enough to hold the four breasts (see the cooking note below) over high heat. Just before the oil begins to smoke, lay the breasts into the pan (away from you so you don't splash oil on yourself). Cook on each side till they're golden brown and delicious-looking, a few minutes per side. While they're cooking, set out a clean wire rack or a plate lined with paper towels.

Remove the finished breasts to the rack or paper towel–lined plate. Allow them to rest for a few minutes before serving. Serve with lemon wedges to squeeze over them if you wish.

NOTE: If you don't have a pan big enough to cook all four breasts at once, preheat your oven to 250°F/120°C and place a baking pan with a rack insert in the oven (the rack will keep the breading on the bottom from getting soggy). You can cook as many as will fit in your pan and keep them warm in the oven for up to 20 minutes (if this is the plan, remove them from the oil as soon as they're golden brown, as they'll keep cooking a bit in the oven). You can cook all four breasts and keep them warm this way while you finish other components of the meal.

Binder

Picadillo Meatballs

MAKES 30 TO 40 (1-OUNCE/30-GRAM) MEATBALLS

Whole eggs can serve as a binding device, and meatballs are the perfect example. Inspired by my friend Annie's love of the meatball shops in Manhattan, and by my friend Nathan's passion for a Cuban stew called picadillo, *I decided to create a spicy meatball that features the egg as both binder and enricher. These meatballs are spiked with chipotle peppers and flavored by annatto seeds, which color the oil a deep red and impart a slightly bitter flavor to balance the sweetness of the onions and peppers. (Annatto seeds can be found in Mexican or Latin grocery stores or specialty spice stores, and in many well-stocked supermarkets.) This recipe will yield four to six meal-size portions—make yellow rice by sautéing some onion in more annatto oil, then adding the rice and liquid—but they also make great hors d'oeuvres, with some hot sauce on the side for dipping.*

Note that annatto oil stains countertops and fingernails, so be sure to lay a large sheet of parchment on your work surface, and manicured ladies may want to don gloves or use a scoop to shape the meatballs (nonpowdered latex gloves are inexpensive and handy to have generally—to wear when cutting hot chile peppers, for instance).

¼ cup/60 milliliters vegetable oil, plus more for pan-frying

3 tablespoons annatto seeds

1 medium red bell pepper, seeded and cut into small dice

1 medium Spanish onion, cut into small dice

4 garlic cloves, minced

2 teaspoons salt

⅓ cup/60 grams pitted, chopped manzanilla olives

¼ cup/30 grams chopped capers

2 chipotle peppers in adobo sauce, seeded and minced

1 pound/450 grams ground beef

1 pound/450 grams ground pork

1 egg, beaten

Flour, for dredging

Hot sauce, for serving

Combine the oil and annatto seeds in a small saucepan over medium heat, bring the oil to a simmer, reduce the heat to medium-low, and continue to cook for about 5 minutes to infuse the oil.

Strain the oil into a sauté pan over medium-high heat, add the pepper, onion, and garlic, and then sprinkle them with 1 teaspoon of the salt. Sauté the vegetables, reducing the heat to medium-low after a minute or two, until they're very tender, 15 minutes or so. Remove the vegetables, along with any residual oil, to a plate and set aside to cool, then cover and refrigerate until completely chilled, 20 to 30 minutes.

In a large mixing bowl, combine the chilled onion-pepper mixture with the olives, capers, chipotle peppers, beef, pork, and egg. Sprinkle it all with the remaining 1 teaspoon salt and mix thoroughly by hand (or use a standing mixer with a paddle attachment, but be aware that the more you paddle, the more tightly bound the meatballs will be when cooked).

Put some flour in a shallow bowl. Form the meat mixture into balls the size of golf balls, dredge them in the flour, and shake off the excess. Pour about ¾ inch/2 centimeters oil into a large skillet over high heat—the oil should come halfway up the sides of the meatballs. When the oil is hot, add as many meatballs as will fit comfortably without crowding, and pan-fry them, rolling them around in the oil until they are nicely browned on all sides and just cooked through, 7 minutes or so. Transfer the cooked meatballs to a wire rack or paper towel–lined plate and continue cooking the remaining meatballs.

Serve with hot sauce.

Custard

CUSTARD IS WITHOUT DOUBT ONE OF THE supreme transformations of the egg. A plain vanilla custard, such as crème caramel, is a textural marvel, quivering on the spoon, delicate on the palate. And a big, thick quiche—which Thomas Keller rightly calls the sexiest pie—is a silky, satiny wonder when baked in a proper 2-inch ring. A custard cooked in a piecrust or tart ring is a different kind of textural experience: the pleasure is in the contrast of the creamy custard and the crunch of the crust. A true fat quiche or sweet vanilla custard is *voluptuous*.

Custards can be sweet or savory. Thick or thin. Served standing alone, or supported by a crust. They can be made with yolks alone, as in crème brûlée, or with whites only, as in panna cotta. The whites are composed mainly of protein, which sets up very solidly, so that a custard made with whole eggs can be sliceable, while one made with only yolks is so creamy and adhering you'd be unable to remove it intact from its cooking vessel.

Custards are also a tool, a binder that can add satisfying fat and flavor. The best bread puddings are simply bread soaked in a flavorful custard and then baked. You can make a sweet custard with cream and cinnamon and sugar and vanilla for a dessert bread pudding, or you can make it savory. Last Thanksgiving, I was in charge of the dressing (we've long stopped stuffing the turkey), and I made a custard using eggs and turkey stock, then poured it over the cubed day-old bread. It made a fabulous, flavorful dressing.

And custard is an easy ratio, as well: two parts liquid to one part egg. Large eggs weigh about 2 ounces/60 grams each. Double that quantity for the liquid, blend, then mix with your ingredients.

Classic French Quiche with Chorizo and Roasted Peppers

SERVES 10 TO 12

I was a youngster in the 1970s when quiche made its appearance on the Midwestern scene, only to be quickly lampooned as girly-man food. It was a time when French food was beginning to make its way into American home kitchens, thanks to Julia Child and the popularity of French restaurants in New York City in the previous decade. But a lot of things got lost in translation. Spinach salad with bacon vinaigrette was the only way we Midwesterners could re-create a classic salade frisée aux lardons. And we cooked quiche in a piecrust—too thin to be of any deep pleasure.

It wasn't until decades later, when I was working with Thomas Keller and Jeffrey Cerciello on the Bouchon *cookbook, that I learned all that a quiche might be. It is little more than an egg pie, a custard pie, but when it's cooked at a proper thickness, it can become utterly seductive. Again, it's all about the power of the egg to transform the ingredients it joins.*

In France, a common quiche is Lorraine, with bacon and onions—and if you're sticking with its peasant roots, no cheese. Or Florentine, with spinach. Here, to show off the versatility of quiche, I'm using sausage, onion, and roasted red peppers. But you can use any flavorings you wish as long as you bake the quiche in a 2-inch/5-centimeter ring mold or cake pan (alas, a springform pan will leak). I treat a quiche like a cake, pressing the dough into a parchment-lined cake pan, so even if it does leak through the crust, you'll still have a thick, creamy quiche. The amount of dough in this recipe will fit a 9-inch/23-centimeter mold with plenty left over for patching should you need it. If you have only an 8-inch/20-centimeter mold, you'll have even more dough left over, which can be frozen for later use, or you can reduce the amounts of the crust ingredients by one-third if you're measuring by weight; you'll also have some custard left over, which can be baked separately in a large ramekin (it will take 20 to 30 minutes to cook).

FOR THE CRUST:

3 cups/420 grams flour

1 cup/225 grams cold or frozen butter, lard, shortening, or any combination thereof, cut into small pieces

½ teaspoon salt

¼ to ½ cup/60 to 120 grams ice water (The quantity depends on the fat—whole butter has water in it so you need only a couple of ounces; shortening and lard do not contain water and thus need more.)

FOR THE QUICHE:

Vegetable oil for sautéing

8 ounces/225 grams cured Spanish chorizo, cut into medium dice

½ Spanish onion, diced

3 teaspoons salt

1 red, orange, or yellow bell pepper, charred, peeled, seeded, and cut into medium dice (see note below on roasting peppers)

2 cups/480 milliliters milk

1 cup/240 milliliters heavy cream

6 eggs

1 teaspoon salt

½ teaspoon freshly ground black pepper

5 to 6 gratings of nutmeg

2 cups/170 grams grated cheddar cheese

To make the crust, combine the flour, fat, and salt in a mixing bowl and rub the fat between your fingers until you have small beads of fat and plenty of pea-sized chunks. Gradually add the ice water and then the salt and mix gently, just until combined—if you work the dough too hard it will become tough. (If you're making a bigger batch, you can use a standing mixer with a paddle attachment, but remember not to paddle too much after you add the water, just enough so that it comes together.) Shape the dough into a disc, wrap in plastic, and refrigerate for at least 15 minutes or up to 24 hours.

The dough can be used raw for some recipes, as with an apple pie (it's enough for a double-crusted pie). But for a quiche or other pie with a liquid batter, you'll need to bake the shell first (known as blind baking).

Preheat the oven to 325°F/165°C. Line a 9-inch/23-centimeter cake pan (or a ring mold placed on a baking sheet) with parchment. Roll the dough into a circle about ¼ inch/6 millimeters thick. Roll it over the rolling pin to lift it and unroll it over the parchment-lined cake pan, pressing the dough into the corners (use a scrap of dough to do this to avoid tearing the dough with your fingers).

To blind bake a crust, you need to fill the shell with something heavy to prevent the bottom from buckling up. Pie weights are made specifically for this, but a layer of aluminum foil and a pound of dried beans or rice reserved for this purpose does the job just as well. Line the bottom of your shell with another layer of parchment, then add the pie weights or beans and bake for 20 minutes. Remove the parchment and the weights or beans and continue baking until the crust is golden brown and cooked through, another 10 to 15 minutes. Cool completely.

To make the quiche, heat 2 teaspoons of the vegetable oil in a sauté pan over medium heat. When hot, add the chorizo and sauté for a few minutes till warm; remove to a plate lined with paper towels. Add the onions to the same pan with the chorizo fat, along with a four-finger pinch of salt, and sauté until softened, about 10 minutes. Add the roasted peppers and stir just to combine (they don't need further cooking). Remove from the heat and add to the plate with the chorizo. (The filling can be made up to 1 day ahead, as can the quiche shell—either raw or blind-baked).

Preheat the oven to 325°F/165°C. Use raw left-over dough to patch any cracks that opened in the quiche shell as it baked. Place it on a baking sheet.

In a large liquid measure or mixing bowl, combine the milk, cream, eggs, salt, pepper, and nutmeg and, using a hand blender, blend until frothy. This can be done in a standing blender as well, though you may need to do it in two batches, depending on the size of your blender. Or you could even mix the batter in a large bowl using a whisk—in this case, beat the eggs first, then add the rest of the ingredients. The idea will be to add the ingredients

in two layers, using the froth to help keep the ingredients suspended.

Layer half of the chorizo mixture into the shell. Pour half of the frothy custard over the mixture. Sprinkle with half of the cheese. Layer with the remaining chorizo mixture. Refroth the batter and pour the rest into the shell. (You may want to put the baking sheet with the quiche shell into the oven and pour the remaining batter into it there so you can get every bit into the shell. You can even let it overflow to make sure it's up to the very top.) Sprinkle the remaining cheese over the top. Bake until the center of the quiche is just set, about 1½ hours (it may take as long as 2 hours, but don't overcook it; there should still be some jiggle in the center when you take it out of the oven).

Allow the quiche to cool, then cover it with plastic wrap and refrigerate until it's completely chilled. The quiche will keep for up to 5 days.

To remove and serve the quiche, use a knife to cut off the top edges of the crust along the rim or simply break them off by hand. Tug the parchment gently and lift the quiche from the cake pan; if using a ring simply press gently on the bottom once the sides are loosened.

Slice and serve cold or, to serve hot, slice and reheat for 15 minutes in a 350°F/180°C oven on lightly oiled parchment or foil, or cover with plastic and microwave for 1 minute.

NOTE: *To roast bell peppers, set them directly over a gas flame and cook all surfaces until they're black. You can also halve them and broil them, cut sides down, till black. Remove them to a paper bag or put in a bowl and cover with plastic wrap till cooled. Remove the charred skin under cold running water. To use, remove the stem and seeds and cut as directed.*

1. / Roll the dough around a rolling pin to transport it to the pan or ring you've lined with parchment.

2. / Use a scrap of dough to press the quiche dough into the corners of the pan or mold.

5. / Spoon the remaining sausage mixture gently over the frothy surface.

6. / Refroth the custard and finish filling the shell.

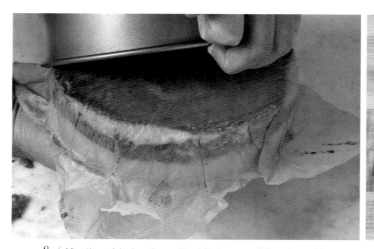

8. / After the quiche has thoroughly chilled, remove it from the mold. If you do so by turning it upside down, that's fine.

9. / The whole quiche can be reheated to serve a group, or individual slices can be cut and served hot or cold.

. / *Place beans on a layer of parchment and bake. About midway through baking, remove the beans and parchment to finish the crust.*

4. / *Put half of the sausage-onion mixture in the bottom of the shell. Pour your very frothy custard over it to about halfway up the pan.*

7. / *The quiche, fresh out of the oven. Allow it to cool, then refrigerate.*

10. / *The quiche is delicious cold, but my favorite way to eat it is hot.*

11. / *Quiche and salad make an enormously satisfying and healthy meal.*

Chawanmushi

SERVES 4

This is a lovely savory custard by one of our key recipe testers, Matthew Kayahara, a French-English translator in Ontario. Matthew spends many off-hours apprenticing at restaurants and cooking at home— particularly Japanese cuisine, since his grandfather was Japanese. This dish—chicken, shrimp, and mushroom bound in a light custard—makes a lovely first course or light meal. The custard uses just enough egg to set the top, but it is so fragile that it breaks as you eat it, and the clarified liquid is almost like a consommé.

Like the Shrimp Tempura (page 141), this recipe calls for dashi, the excellent all-purpose Japanese stock made from kombu seaweed and bonito flakes. It also uses a little sake, so little it's not worth using an expensive one, unless you're also drinking it with the meal. Matthew's preference for everyday use is sake made by Hakutsuru, which is drinkable and reasonably priced. As for the soy sauce, if you can find the light-colored Japanese usukuchi shoyu, *use that.*

2 ounces/60 grams chicken thigh
or breast meat, cut into ½-inch dice

1 teaspoon sake

1 tablespoon plus 1 teaspoon soy sauce

4 small or 2 large shrimp, peeled and
deveined, halved lengthwise if large

A few mushroom pieces for each serving (enoki,
maitake, shiitake, cut bite-size as necessary)

2 eggs

1½ cups/360 milliliters dashi (page 141)

2 teaspoons mirin

½ teaspoon salt

½ scallion, sliced feather-thin on the diagonal,
or 4 small watercress sprigs, for garnish

Grated lemon zest, for garnish (optional)

Combine the diced chicken with the sake and 1 teaspoon of the soy sauce in a small bowl and marinate for 15 minutes. Drain.

Divide the chicken, shrimp, and mushrooms among four 4- to 5-ounce/120- to 150-milliliter ramekins.

In a medium bowl, beat the eggs until smooth. Add the dashi, remaining 1 tablespoon soy sauce, mirin, and salt, and stir to combine well. Divide the mixture among the ramekins. Cover each ramekin with foil.

Place a rack or steamer basket in a pot large enough to hold all four ramekins. Pour in enough water to just reach the rack and bring it to a boil over high heat. Once the water is boiling vigorously, reduce the heat to medium-high, add the ramekins, cover the pot, and steam until the custard is set but still jiggly and the chicken and shrimp are cooked through, 15 to 17 minutes. Carefully remove the foil from the ramekins, garnish each with the scallions or watercress, cover the pot again, and steam until the garnish is just wilted, about 1 more minute. Remove the ramekins, grate a little lemon zest over each if desired, and serve immediately.

Crème Caramel

SERVES 4

This is one of my favorite desserts, notable for its simplicity and elegance. A quick caramel of cooked sugar is poured into a dish and cooled till it's as hard as candy. Then custard is poured into the dish and cooked in a water bath. The liquid custard sets but also transforms the hardened caramel into a sweet syrup that releases from the dish and runs down the sides of the custard. It's a great dessert for a dinner party because it can be made ahead of time and is easy to serve. It is usually prepared in individual ramekins, but it can also be made in a large baking dish, to be served family style, which is how the young Thomas Keller prepared and served it when he was chef at La Rive in New York's Hudson Valley in the early 1980s, a decade before opening the French Laundry in California's Napa Valley.

I prefer my crème caramel straightforward, adhering to its simple roots—a milk custard flavored with vanilla only—though you could infuse it with aromatics, as I do for the Orange-Ginger Panna Cotta (page 187). If you want a richer custard, substitute half-and-half for half of the milk.

FOR THE CARAMEL:

½ cup/100 grams sugar

2 tablespoons water

FOR THE CUSTARD:

2 cups/480 milliliters milk

4 eggs

½ cup/100 grams sugar

Seeds scraped from 1 vanilla bean or 2 teaspoons pure vanilla extract

¼ teaspoon salt

To make the caramel, combine the sugar and water in a small pan over medium heat and cook until the sugar has melted and the mixture turns an appealing shade of brown, gently swirling the sugar (you can stir but do so gently or else the sugar may crystallize). If it foams up, take it off the heat and let it calm down so that you can evaluate the color and doneness. Pour the caramel into four 4- to 5-ounce/120- to 150-milliliter ramekins; it should coat the bottom to about ⅛ inch/3 millimeters. Allow it to cool completely into a hard candy.

Preheat the oven to 325°F/165°C.

Place the ramekins in a large roasting pan and pour water into the pan so that it comes three-quarters of the way up the sides of the ramekins. Remove the ramekins and place the pan of water in the oven.

Combine the custard ingredients and blend them till the mixture is uniform (this can be done with a whisk, a hand blender, or a standing blender, but the whisk is best so that you don't get too much froth). Divide the custard evenly among the ramekins. Place the ramekins in the water bath in the oven. Bake until the custards are almost set, with just a little jiggle at the center, 30 to 40 minutes. Remove them to a rack to cool, then cover the ramekins and refrigerate until thoroughly chilled, several hours at least.

To serve, use the tip of a knife to loosen the edges where the custard adheres to the ramekin and invert them onto plates. Serve immediately.

Basic Bread Pudding (and French Toast)

BREAD PUDDING IS NOTHING MORE THAN A custard poured over bread and baked. When you remember that a custard is two parts liquid and one part egg, then you have a simple and delicious formula to use up leftover bread for either a savory dish, as with Thanksgiving dressing, or a sweet dessert. Bread pudding is especially good when made with leftover Challah (page 93) or Brioche (page 92). And French toast is essentially the same thing—bread soaked in a custard mixture—then sautéed in butter or oil.

This preparation depends on how much bread you have and how many people you need to serve. For each serving, plan on about 1 cup/90 grams stale bread cubes and 6 ounces/170 grams custard (1 egg, ½ cup/120 milliliters milk or half-and-half, 1 to 2 tablespoons sugar, plus flavoring such as vanilla or citrus zest). For savory versions, omit the sugar and replace the dairy with stock or flavor the dairy with sautéed onions, then top the custard-soaked bread with grated cheese.

Bourbon Brioche Bread Pudding

SERVES 6 TO 8

This is a delicious boozy variation on classic bread pudding, using a full loaf of rich brioche.

1½ cups/360 milliliters heavy cream

1 cup/240 milliliters milk

½ cup/120 milliliters bourbon

6 eggs

1¼ packed cups/250 grams dark brown sugar

1 teaspoon pure vanilla extract

1 teaspoon ground cinnamon

½ teaspoon ground nutmeg

¼ teaspoon salt

Pinch of cayenne pepper

10 cups diced brioche (1-inch/2.5-centimeter dice), left out overnight or baked in a 200°F/95°C oven till dry

Preheat the oven to 350°F/180°C.

In a large mixing bowl, combine all of the ingredients except the brioche cubes. Whisk until well combined.

Add the brioche cubes and toss them in the liquid, pressing them down so they absorb it. Allow the mixture to sit for 1 hour.

Butter a 9-inch (23-centimeter) square baking pan or standard loaf pan. Press the mixture into the pan.

Bake until a toothpick inserted into the center comes out clean, about 1 hour. Slice and serve with Crème Anglaise (page 171) or your favorite ice cream.

Almond Challah French Toast

SERVES 4 TO 8

If you don't have leftover challah, then you haven't made enough! But neither do you want to waste it. Wrapped in foil, challah freezes well, but a better use is simply to slice it thick and let the pieces dry overnight, then use it to make a delicious breakfast by soaking it in a tasty custard mixture—here equal parts egg and liquid—and then sautéing it. These finish in the oven, so it's an easy dish to serve to a hungry family. You can certainly slather this French toast in butter and maple syrup, but if you want to make it an especially extravagant plate, I suggest serving it with toasted almonds, whipped cream, and a simple cherry sauce.

¾ cup/180 milliliters half-and-half

3 eggs

2 tablespoons kirsch

2 tablespoons sugar

1 teaspoon pure almond extract

1 teaspoon ground cinnamon

Pinch of ground nutmeg

Pinch of salt

6 to 8 thick (1 inch/2.5 centimeters) slices challah, left out overnight or baked in a 200°F/95°C oven till dry

Vegetable oil for pan-frying

Cherry Sauce (recipe below), for serving

¾ cup/180 milliliters whipping cream, whipped to firm peaks, for serving

½ cup/54 grams toasted slivered almonds, for serving

Preheat the oven to 325°F/165°C.

In a shallow mixing bowl, combine the half-and-half, eggs, kirsch, sugar, almond extract, cinnamon, nutmeg, and salt. Whisk until well combined.

Place the challah slices in the batter for 5 minutes, then flip to the other side.

Heat a large sauté pan over medium-high heat with a coating of vegetable oil. Working in batches, remove the challah slices from the batter and fry them until golden brown, roughly 3 minutes per side, then transfer them to a baking sheet.

Once all of the slices are cooked, bake them for 10 minutes.

Serve with the warm cherry sauce, whipped cream, and toasted almonds.

Cherry Sauce

MAKES 2 CUPS/480 MILLILITERS

2 cups/250 grams sweet cherries, pitted and halved

¼ cup/50 grams sugar

¼ cup/60 milliliters plus 2 teaspoons water

Pinch of salt

A few drops of fresh lemon juice

1 teaspoon cornstarch

2 tablespoons kirsch

In a small pot combine the cherries, sugar, ¼ cup of the water, and the salt and bring to a simmer over medium-high heat. Add the lemon juice and allow to cook for a few minutes more.

Put the cornstarch in a small bowl and stir in the remaining 2 teaspoons water to make a slurry. Pour the slurry into the cherry mixture and simmer until the sauce has thickened, 20 to 30 seconds, then remove it from the heat. Stir in the kirsch.

Serve warm, poured over the French toast.

Enricher

Nineteenth-Century Ale and Rum Flip

SERVES 1

Flips, combining ale, rum, and sugar, may have originated with British sailors; the term flip *refers to the froth created. Some descriptions are of hot flips, heated with the insertion of a red-hot poker, which would have generated froth. Eggs appear to have been introduced in Jerry Thomas's nineteenth-century book* How to Mix Drinks. *Today's flips are typically sherry based. This cocktail is practically a meal in itself and a great libation to serve hot or cold, but I prefer it hot. Instead of adding my own spices, I simply use a spiced ale, which is ubiquitous around the winter holidays. This recipe makes one flip; if you're serving a group (which you should), use a standing blender.*

3 ounces/85 milliliters spiced Christmas or pumpkin ale

2 ounces/55 milliliters dark rum

1 egg

Pinch of ground coriander (or whole coriander seeds shaved on a Microplane) or ground ginger (optional)

Grated orange zest (optional)

Combine the ale, rum, and egg in a large mug. Whisk or blend with a hand mixer. Or toss the drink back and forth between two large mugs, as Jerry Thomas might have done. Heat it for 40 to 50 seconds in the microwave (or use a red-hot poker). If desired, top with a pinch of coriander or ginger and some grated orange zest.

Part Four

The Dough-Batter Continuum

It was as close to a spiritual revelation as I've had when writing about food. I was at work on *Ratio: The Simple Codes Behind the Craft of Everyday Cooking,* which looks at basic food preparations—bread, cake, stock, custard, sauces—in terms of the proportions of their key ingredients, the ingredients without which they would cease to be what they are. That is, I didn't concern myself with how much curry was in the mayonnaise but rather with the ratio of oil to water and yolk that made the mayonnaise *mayonnaise.* You need some yeast for leavening and salt for flavor in a bread, but what is critical is the ratio of the flour to the water. It doesn't matter what flavorings go into a muffin—cranberries or chocolate chips or walnuts—but rather the architecture of the muffin itself, equal parts flour and liquid by weight, half as much egg and butter. Which is basically what pancake batter is, whether plain or flavored with bananas or blueberries, just poured onto a flat hot surface rather than into a muffin tin. And then I realized that if you poured pancake batter over corn or peas, just to coat, and then fried them, you'd have a fritter. And that if you simply added more liquid to your fritter batter you had crêpe batter, not muffin-pancake-fritter batter.

So in my head, over a period of about twenty minutes, I'd gone from a dense bread dough to a loose crêpe batter, and it occurred to me that these preparations were essentially the same thing except for how much liquid they contained. It's an important fact for all cooks to know. There are, of course, small differences, most notably the quantity of fat used. For instance, I use more fat in muffins or quick breads than in pancakes; and since fritters are cooked in tons of fat you don't really need to add fat to the batter—it's the liquid-egg-flour combo that makes it what it is. What's critical here is the mighty role that eggs play in this continuum—so critical that I'm devoting a whole section to the range of flour-liquid preparations that rely on egg for their existence.

It is obvious that the egg is essential to egg salad, or eggs Benedict, or a fried-egg sandwich, but it is equally essential when hidden within a wide range of preparations, its effects at once beguiling and wondrous. Challah isn't challah without the egg, for example. A crêpe batter without egg is paste.

Because I'd like to move from dough to batter, stiff to loose, we begin with the great egg breads.

Brioche and challah are distinguished from one another—that is, made what they are—by the egg and the fat. Whole eggs are used in brioche; challah can be made with whole eggs or yolks only. The addition of eggs makes both doughs rich and flavorful; take out the eggs and they become other types of bread entirely. The brioche gets its tender crumb from the fat added to the dough; the fat prevents the gluten from forming, resulting in a cakelike bread. The challah uses less fat, so it is chewier than brioche; it tears rather than breaks or crumbles. Each bread is simple to make, the most basic of foods, comprising fundamental ingredients: flour, water, salt, yeast, egg, and fat. The classic brioche is made with luxurious butter, though there's no reason why you can't use any fat, such as olive oil or, as in one of my recent projects, *The Book of Schmaltz*, rendered chicken fat, which results in a splendid savory brioche.

• • •

Ingredient/Tool

Brioche

MAKES 1 (2-POUND/900-GRAM) LOAF

I created this bread for my daughter, who, at an early age, adored the tender richness of brioche. I used my trusty New Professional Chef *as my guide, the CIA textbook that I remain devoted to (despite the fact that it calls for 5 pounds of flour, 26 eggs, and 3½ pounds of sugar—not exactly home-kitchen friendly; also it uses fresh yeast, which I no longer use*). This brioche is a staple in our house for Christmas morning, and the leftover loaf can be frozen for a week and eaten sliced and toasted with foie gras to celebrate the New Year. Extra, left out to dry, will make outstanding French toast (page 86) or bread pudding (page 85).*

¼ cup/60 milliliters milk

¼ cup/75 grams honey

1 teaspoon/7 grams instant dry yeast

3 cups/420 grams bread flour

6 eggs

¼ cup/50 grams sugar

½ teaspoon salt

1½ cups/340 grams butter, cut into 12 pieces and brought to room temperature

Combine the milk, honey, and yeast in the bowl of a standing mixer and stir until the yeast is dissolved. Add about one-quarter of the flour and mix it well with the dough hook. Allow this mixture to sit for 1 hour to ferment.

Add the eggs, sugar, salt, and the remaining flour. Mix until the dough forms and pulls cleanly from the sides of the bowl.

Add the butter, one chunk at a time, until it's all been incorporated and a smooth, soft dough forms. Cover the mixing bowl with plastic wrap and let it rise to double its volume, 2 to 4 hours depending on the temperature of the kitchen.

Turn the dough out onto a floured surface and knead it to deflate the dough and redistribute the yeast. Shape it to fit in whatever mold you are using (anything from a terrine mold to a traditional bread-baking dish), cover loosely with plastic, and refrigerate overnight.

Remove the dough from the refrigerator 1 to 2 hours before baking. Preheat the oven to 350°F/180°C. Bake until the crust is golden brown and the dough is cooked through (the interior temperature should read around 200°F/95°C on an instant-read thermometer), about 45 minutes.

---

* The quality of dry yeast is now very good and most bakers rely on it. I prefer Red Star or SAF instant dried yeast, which is just slightly stronger than active dried yeast; use either, as they work more or less the same.

Challah

MAKES 1 (1½-POUND/680-GRAM) LOAF

Challah is among the most delectable breads you can make and is very easy to do at home. It derives its great color, texture, and flavor from the egg, in this case whole eggs. Challah doesn't have nearly as much fat as brioche, but it has some. My preferred fat is schmaltz— chicken fat and skin rendered with onion—which is what would have been added in the Ashkenazi Jewish culinary tradition from which challah derives (it's traditionally eaten on the Sabbath and at the two primary holiday times of the year). This fat gives the challah a great depth of flavor. Butter is my second choice. The dough should be mixed a day before baking, which helps it develop flavor. If you want a gigantic, celebratory six-braid bread, you'll need to weigh out your ingredients (which you should do anyhow) and double them. I'll explain how to create a three-braid loaf (see photos on pages 94–95), but there are many good videos and pictorials online that demonstrate how to braid larger loaves.

3½ cups/490 grams flour

¼ cup/50 grams sugar

2 tablespoons honey

1 tablespoon/21 grams instant dry yeast (or 3 tablespoons/63 grams if you'd like to bake the bread on the same day you mix it)

7 eggs

¼ cup/60 grams butter or schmaltz, at room temperature

1 tablespoon salt

2 tablespoons sesame seeds or poppy seeds, for garnish (optional)

In the bowl of a standing mixer fitted with a dough hook, combine the flour, sugar, honey, yeast, and 6 of the eggs. Mix on medium until the dough comes together. Add the butter and continue to mix. Add the salt. Mix until the dough is well kneaded, 8 to 10 minutes in all. Turn the dough out onto a floured board and knead for a minute or so by hand to develop more structure. Put the dough into a bowl wiped with vegetable or olive oil.

Cover the bowl and refrigerate overnight or, if you want to bake it that day, cover and let it rise at room temperature for a few hours (it won't quite double in size).

Turn the dough out onto a floured board. Knead it to press out air and redistribute the yeast. Divide the dough into three equal pieces (about 300 grams apiece; weighing the dough will ensure accuracy) and shape them into rectangles. Cover the dough pieces with a towel and let them rest for 30 minutes.

To shape the bread, fold the top of each rectangle down, sealing it with the heel of your hand as you do. Continue sealing until you have a squat cylinder, then roll the dough to elongate it so that it's about 12 to 14 inches/31 to 36 centimeters long.

For a three-braid challah, work from the middle out. Set the pieces parallel on a cutting board or a piece of parchment paper. Put the center of the top piece over the middle piece. Put the center of the bottom piece over the center of the top piece (which is crossing the middle piece). Now, finish this half of the bread by folding the top piece into the center, followed by the bottom piece, until you reach the end, pinching the three tips together.

Turn the dough around and do the same to the other side. Whip the last egg till it's uniformly mixed and brush the dough with it; reserve the remaining egg wash. Allow the dough to rise for 1 hour.

Put a baking sheet or baking stone in the oven and preheat the oven to 350°F/180°C.

Brush the dough again with egg wash and transfer the dough, on the parchment paper, to the baking sheet or stone in the oven. Bake until cooked through (the interior temperature should read around 200°F/95°C on an instant-read thermometer), about 40 minutes. It should be gorgeously brown and shiny on top. Allow it to cool for at least 30 minutes before cutting.

I. / *When the dough has risen, turn out onto a floured board and knead to deflate it and redistribute the yeast.*

4. / *After rolling out the three cylinders till they're about 12 inches long, lay them parallel on a cutting board or piece of parchment.*

6. / *After pinching the ends together, rotate your board 180 degrees and braid the remaining half of the loaf.*

2. / Divide the dough in thirds and shape them into rectangles.

3. / Fold the top of each cylinder down by an inch or two and seal with the heel of your hand. Continue sealing until you have a squat cylinder.

5. / Working from the center out, cross the top piece over the middle one, the bottom piece over the top, and repeat.

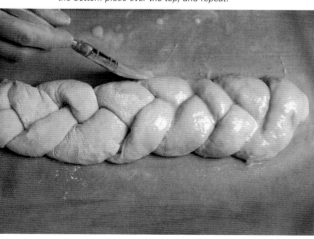

7. / Brush the dough with egg wash. Feel free to sprinkle the loaf with sesame seeds or poppy seeds after brushing.

8. / The finished dough should be light and rich, and the crust appealing and golden-brown.

All-Purpose Pasta

SERVES 4

Needless to say, making your own pasta is more time-consuming than cracking open a cardboard box and dumping the contents into boiling water. But dry pasta—and, indeed, even "fresh" pasta sold in stores—is a different product than what you can make on your own. (It's also a lot more fun, if you like to cook.) As with homemade mayonnaise, you simply cannot buy anything like what you can make at home, which is reason enough to make it. Also, it's not that difficult if you plan ahead, clear your work surface, and stay organized. When you make your own pasta, not only is it better tasting, but it allows you to cut it to whatever shape you wish—fettuccine, tagliatelle, or flat sheets for ravioli or lasagna. I worked for a chef who rolled big sheets of cooked pasta around pastry cream for a pasta dessert, slicing off portions as if it were a tortilla sandwich wrap.

Pasta can be made with just flour and water, but add whole egg to the equation and it becomes a flavorful wonder. The flour needs some water to create the gluten that allows it to become elastic, but there's enough water in the egg itself to cover this duty. Again, weighing your ingredients is highly recommended, but you can always adjust the consistency of your pasta dough by adding water if it's too stiff or more flour if it's too sticky (try to avoid the former, because it's harder to incorporate liquid into a stiff dough than flour into a wet one).

Once again, egg turns ordinary flour into a heavenly food. And frankly, it doesn't matter what flour you use. The hunger for homemade noodles usually strikes me from out of the blue, and because all-purpose is always on hand in my house, that's what I use. But if you have access to finely ground "00" Italian flour, terrific. Want to try the high-protein semolina flour from durum wheat? Go for it. You'll find various recipes out there, but it boils down to a basic ratio of three parts flour to two parts egg by weight. Using a kitchen scale makes this a breeze. If you don't have one, figure on a generous ½ cup flour per egg per serving.

I have a pasta roller, but I find that my 4-foot-long pasta rolling pin is the easiest, fastest, and cleanest method (a standard rolling pin can be used as well). The thinner you roll the dough, the better, as it does expand and thicken when cooked.

2½ cups/350 grams flour

4 eggs

In a mixing bowl, combine the flour and eggs and stir till the eggs are incorporated. When the dough is kneadable, turn it out onto a work surface and knead until all of the flour is incorporated into the dough and the dough is luxuriously smooth (this should take about 10 minutes, the cook's version of transcendental meditation). Shape the dough into a rectangle about 1 inch/2.5 centimeters thick, cover with a kitchen towel, and let rest at room temperature for at least 20 minutes, or wrap it in plastic and refrigerate for up to a day.

Cut the dough into thirds and roll it using a machine. Or, if you have a pasta rolling pin, search online for any of numerous videos demonstrating how to roll; still photos can't capture the technique required as you roll, pressing both down and out to stretch the dough. You'll need to roll patiently, as the dough will resist you (part of its goodness in the end), and allow it to rest as needed.

Cut as desired and cook in boiling salted water until done, 3 to 5 minutes, depending on the size and shape.

1. / *The easiest, cleanest way to make pasta is to weigh your eggs before adding the appropriate amount of flour.*

2. / *The ideal pasta dough is a 2:3 egg-flour ratio (e.g., 6 ounces egg and 9 ounces flour, or 200 grams egg and 300 grams flour).*

5. / *Knead the dough into itself (the yolks make it very sticky).*

6. / *Continue kneading until the dough is smooth and no longer sticky, about 10 minutes. Take a moment to reflect on the lovely texture.*

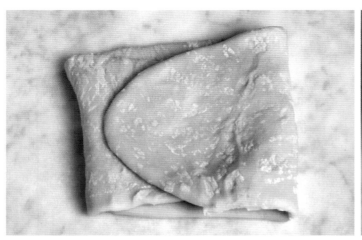

9. / *Fold each piece in thirds so that it matches the maximum width of the machine and roll it through the largest setting again. Repeat with all the pieces.*

10. / *Roll each piece through consecutively thinner settings.*

3. / *I begin mixing the dough in a bowl because the traditional method of adding eggs to a well of flour can be messy if the eggs overflow the well.*

4. / *Once the egg is incorporated, dump the dough onto a work surface.*

7. / *Divide the dough in thirds.*

8. / *Run each piece of dough through the largest setting of a pasta machine.*

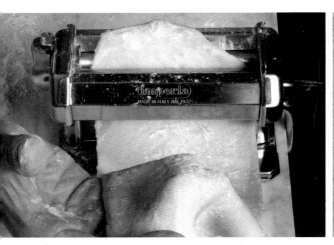

11. / *As the pasta gets thinner and thinner, add more flour as necessary to prevent sticking.*

12. / *The rolled pasta can now be cut to whatever shape you wish.*

Yolk-Only Pasta

SERVES 2 TO 4

In years of writing about, and for, chefs, as well as cooking and hanging out in kitchens, I've found that certain odd bits of information catch in the brain and remain stuck there. During Thomas Keller's travels in Italy, he worked in a kitchen in the Piedmont region where he learned to make the ingenious self-sealing ravioli called agnolotti. *But what stuck with me was his comment about how every chef wanted to see how many yolks he could get into a kilo of flour. The general consensus was thirty. Here I'll make the ratio even easier: one part flour to three-quarters part yolk, with olive oil to ease the stickiness (so if you're using a scale to weigh out your flour, multiply that weight by 0.75 for the weight of yolks required; or weigh out the yolks and multiply it by 1.33 to determine the weight of the flour).*

Yolk-only dough results in a delicious, rich pasta, excellent for ravioli or agnolotti or simply cut as spaghetti and finished with some excellent olive oil. Unlike whole-egg pasta dough, this yolk-only dough—via chefs Michael Symon and Marc Vetri—requires very little kneading, just enough to bring it all together. But it does require a pasta roller, which serves as the kneading device. I find this dough to be so dry and flaky that I don't need extra flour or cornmeal to keep it from sticking, but it depends on your environment; use your common sense. If you have access to very finely ground "00" Italian flour, use that, but all-purpose will work fine.

1½ cups/210 grams flour

8 to 10 egg yolks

1 tablespoon flavorful extra-virgin olive oil

Combine all of the ingredients in a bowl and stir to mix. Pour out onto a work surface and knead the dough just till it comes together. Shape it into a rectangle about ½ inch/1 centimeter thick, cover it with a kitchen towel, and let it rest for 20 to 30 minutes.

Cut the dough in half and roll it through the widest setting of your machine several times. Then decrease the width by one click and continue to roll until you've reached the penultimate setting. Cut as desired.

Cook in boiling water (which you've salted until it tastes seasoned) until the pasta is tender, 3 to 5 minutes, depending on the size and shape.

Italian Drop Cookies with Lemon Glaze

MAKES 20 LARGE OR 40 SMALL COOKIES

Here I put the egg into action to make cookies. The richness of the dough comes from the yolks, and the water in the egg allows some gluten to form, giving the cookies a cakey bite rather than the crumbly texture of a shortbread-style cookie. These are not sweet cookies, but they get sweetness from a finishing lemony glaze.

FOR THE COOKIES:

½ cup/100 grams granulated sugar

¼ cup/60 grams unsalted butter, at room temperature

Zest and juice of ½ lemon

3 eggs

2 cups/280 grams flour

2 teaspoons baking powder

¼ teaspoon salt

FOR THE GLAZE:

2½ cups/250 grams confectioners' sugar

¼ cup/60 milliliters fresh lemon juice

Zest of 1 lemon

Preheat the oven to 350°F/180°C.

Combine the sugar, butter, and lemon zest in a standing mixer and paddle on medium-high till thoroughly creamed, about 5 minutes. Reduce the speed to medium and add the eggs one by one while paddling, followed by the lemon juice.

In a small mixing bowl, whisk together the flour, baking powder (press it through a strainer if it's chunky), and salt. Add the dry ingredients to the egg-butter mixture while paddling, just till the dough comes together. The dough should be pale yellow and sticky.

Line a baking sheet with a Silpat or parchment paper. Using two spoons to scrape the dough off each other, drop the sticky cookie dough onto the lined baking sheet. You can make the cookies teaspoon- or tablespoon-size. Leave about 2 inches/ 5 centimeters between the cookies; they will spread a bit.

Bake until the cookies are lightly browned, 10 to 12 minutes. Remove the cookies from the oven and transfer them to a wire rack to cool.

To make the glaze, in a small bowl, whisk together the confectioners' sugar, lemon juice, and half of the zest until the sugar is completely dissolved. The icing should be nearly a paste that falls in ribbons when you lift the whisk from the bowl.

When the cookies are cool, hold each one by the edges and dunk just the very top in the glaze. Once they're glazed, place the cookies on a wire rack to allow any excess glaze to drip off. Garnish with the remaining zest while the glaze is still soft and not yet set.

Norwegian Berlinerkranser

MAKES ABOUT 40 COOKIES

My assistant Emilia, a true cookie hound, sent me this recipe. I found it irresistible for its use of whole eggs and also two hard-cooked yolks, which I've never seen elsewhere. These are crisp shortbread-style cookies, enriched with the yolk and shaped into folded ribbons before baking.

2 hard-cooked egg yolks

2 eggs, separated

½ cup/60 grams sugar

1 cup/225 grams butter, cut into chunks and brought to room temperature

Pinch of salt

2 cups/280 grams flour

Pearl or decorating sugar, for garnish

Preheat the oven to 350°F/180°C.

Press the hard-cooked yolks through a sieve into the bowl of a standing mixer. Add the raw egg yolks and sugar to the sieved yolks. Using the paddle attachment, beat on medium-high speed until smooth, light, and creamy, about 5 minutes.

Paddle about one-quarter of the butter into the yolk batter. Once combined, add the salt, then add the remaining butter and the flour alternately, until the ingredients come together into a tight ball. This will become a very thick dough.

Scrape the dough out onto a sheet of plastic wrap. Form the dough into a rectangle 10 inches/25 centimeters long, 4 to 5 inches/10 to 12 centimeters wide, and ⅜ inch/1 centimeter thick. Cover with another sheet of plastic, wrap tightly, and refrigerate for at least an hour or overnight.

Slice the dough crosswise into strips about 3/16 inch/5 millimeters thick. Roll the strips into cylinders about 3/16 inch/5 millimeters thick and 6 inches/15 centimeters long. Form each cylinder into a loop and cross the ends over each other. Place the cookies on two parchment- or Silpat-lined baking sheets, spacing them about 2 inches/5 centimeters apart. Brush the tops with the egg whites and sprinkle with pearl sugar.

Bake until slightly golden, 12 to 15 minutes. Transfer to a wire rack to cool.

Gougères

MAKES ABOUT 24 GOUGÈRES

Cheese puffs are the savory version of cream puffs (or profiteroles, which follow). They're passed around at wine tastings, popped into the mouth without a thought—but mmm, so good. Truly these little creations are one of the great manifestations of how the egg unites the fundamental ingredients of our kitchen—butter, flour, and water—and transforms them into airy little wonders. Take away the egg and you've got a projectile—"lethal when thrown," according to a professional baker on Twitter.

Despite the elegant results, the preparation is simple and also unique in that the flour is first cooked in the water and butter, then the eggs are whipped in. Then this dough-batter hybrid can be baked (it puffs!), deep-fried, or boiled, all with different and wonderful results.

But here we simply want puffballs. One part water and half as much butter is brought to a simmer; an amount of flour equal to the weight of the butter is then stirred in. The flour absorbs the water and begins to gel, but it is also shortened by the butter (that is, gluten is prevented from forming, which results in tenderness). Next, eggs are whipped into this paste, the yolks giving their richness to it, the whites eventually spreading out to trap steam as the paste bakes. This is basic pâte à choux *dough. The dough is piped into balls and popped into a very hot oven. They begin to puff as the water expands into steam, but the exterior crusts over while the creamy interior—the starch gelling, the egg-white proteins setting—continues to expand. The oven temperature is lowered so that the exterior crust doesn't overcook or burn before the interior is fully set. The result is a delectable puff.*

How to make them even easier? Pipe out the balls, freeze them, then pop them in the oven whenever you want them.

Now the question becomes how to flavor them. Gougères are flavored with cheese, typically Gruyère, Emmentaler, or Comté. Chef Shuna Fish Lydon, who has made thousands, probably tens of thousands, of gougères, feels that because they are a French preparation, one should use only a French cheese (Comté). I say we're in America, a melting pot, so it's fine to add a little Parmigiano-Reggiano to the mix, and cheddar would surely work as well. If you want to take this one step further, pipe a cheese sauce into the hollow puffs. (See Quail Eggs Croque Madame, page 34, for the Mornay sauce recipe, increasing the amount of flour by a few tablespoons.)

1 cup/240 milliliters water

½ cup/110 grams butter

½ teaspoon salt

1 scant cup/130 grams flour

4 eggs

1 cup/120 grams grated Gruyère
(or other cheese noted above)

½ cup/50 grams grated Parmigiano-Reggiano

Preheat the oven to 425F°/220°C. Line a baking sheet with parchment paper or a Silpat and set aside.

Combine the water, butter, and salt in a small saucepan and bring the water to a simmer over high heat. When the butter has melted, add the flour, lower the heat to medium-low, and stir continuously until a paste forms, about 30 seconds. Continue to cook and stir for another 30 seconds.

To get maximum rise, transfer the paste to a standing mixer fitted with the paddle attachment, and paddle on medium-high, adding one egg at a time. Or, leaving the paste in the saucepan, stir in the eggs one at a time with a wooden spoon, vigorously, till incorporated. Add the Gruyère and half the Parmigiano and paddle or stir till incorporated.

Transfer the mixture to a pastry bag fitted with a ½-inch/1.25-centimeter straight tip (or use a sturdy plastic bag, cutting a ½-inch/1.25-centimeter hole at the corner). Pipe out 1½-inch/4-centimeter orbs of paste onto the prepared baking sheet, leaving an inch or two between them. With a wet finger tap down any tips that you may have left from the piping. Sprinkle each orb with a little of the remaining Parmigiano. (The raw puffs can be frozen like this, then dumped into a plastic bag and stored in the freezer for up to a month. You may want to add more cheese before baking.) Slide the baking sheet into the oven.

Bake for 10 minutes, then lower the heat to 350°F/180°C and continue to bake till cooked inside, 25 to 30 minutes more (you'll have to sacrifice one to yourself to know for sure whether they're done). Serve within the hour.

Profiteroles with Vanilla Ice Cream and Chocolate

MAKES ABOUT 24 PROFITEROLES, SERVES 8

Profiteroles are simply the sweet version of gougères. *I use milk instead of water, and a little sugar instead of salt. There's no reason you couldn't infuse the milk with vanilla beans if you want to up the flavor.*

A traditional French bistro dessert is profiteroles with vanilla ice cream and chocolate sauce. Because these puffs are largely hollow, they are often filled with pastry cream (cream puffs). And elaborate statues composed of profiteroles are often created by sticking them together with caramel; these structures are called croquembouches.

As with gougères, *you can pipe these out several weeks in advance and freeze them, making them great for last-minute desserts and great for entertaining. For an all-homemade dessert, go all out and make Vanilla Ice Cream (page 173) and Chocolate Glaze (page 130), or throw together a quick chocolate sauce by pouring piping-hot cream over an equal amount of chopped chocolate, waiting a few minutes and whisking to satiny uniformity.*

1 cup/240 milliliters milk

½ cup /110 grams butter

1 tablespoon sugar

1 scant cup/130 grams flour

4 eggs

Preheat the oven to 425°F/220°C. Line a baking sheet with parchment paper or a Silpat and set aside.

Combine the milk, butter, and sugar in a small saucepan and bring to a simmer over high heat. When the butter has melted, add the flour, lower the heat to medium-low, and stir continuously until a paste forms, about 30 seconds. Continue to cook and stir for another 30 seconds.

To get maximum rise, transfer the paste to a standing mixer fitted with the paddle attachment, and paddle on medium-high, adding one egg at a time. Or, leaving the paste in the saucepan, stir in the eggs one at a time with a wooden spoon, vigorously, till incorporated.

Transfer the mixture to a pastry bag fitted with a ½-inch/1.25-centimeter straight tip (or use a sturdy plastic bag, cutting a ½-inch/1.25-centimeter hole at the corner). Pipe out 1½-inch/4-centimeter orbs of paste onto the prepared baking sheet, leaving an inch or two between them. With a wet finger, tap down any tips that you may have left from the piping. (The raw puffs can be frozen like this, then dumped into a plastic bag and stored in the freezer for a month at this point.) Slide the baking sheet into the oven.

Bake for 10 minutes, then lower the heat to 350°F/180°C and continue to bake till cooked inside, 25 to 30 minutes more (you'll have to sacrifice one to yourself to know for sure whether they're done). Serve within the hour.

To finish the dessert:

12 profiteroles

1 cup/240 milliliters Vanilla Ice Cream (page 173)

1 cup/240 milliliters Chocolate Glaze (page 130)

Halve each profiterole through the equator (to make ice cream sandwiches) and place three on each plate. Scoop ice cream onto the bottoms of the profiteroles, put the tops on, and finish each by drizzling warm chocolate sauce over the profiteroles.

Crisp and Fluffy Potato Pancakes

SERVES 4

One of the great uses for pâte à choux, *the eggy cooked flour dough-batter, is that when added to leftover mashed potatoes, it creates sensational potato pancakes unlike any other. The* choux *paste serves as a binder and a leavener, once again thanks to the egg and the trapping of expanding steam. As you should make mashed potatoes often, and always enough so that you have leftovers, you should be able to make these potato pancakes regularly. Use an equal volume of potatoes and* pâte à choux *for the pancakes and sauté. I like them very crispy, so I press both sides in panko bread crumbs before sautéing. It's not necessary, but I love the contrasting crunch. Marlene Newell, chief recipe tester, begged me to include herbs and cheese to further amp up the flavor. OK, bend my arm.*

1 cup/240 milliliters mashed potatoes

1 cup/240 milliliters *pâte à choux*
(½ recipe, page 103)

Salt

2 scallions, finely chopped (all the white and some green), or 4 tablespoons minced fresh chives

¼ cup/30 grams grated cheddar cheese (optional)

About 1 cup panko

Vegetable oil for sautéing

Salt and freshly ground black pepper

Stir together the mashed potatoes and *pâte à choux*, salting to taste, along with the scallions and cheese, if using, until they're uniformly distributed. Shape into patties as desired. You should have about eight 3-inch/7.5-centimeter pancakes. Press both sides of each pancake into the panko.

Pour about ¼ inch/6 millimeters oil into a large sauté pan over medium-high heat. When the oil is hot, add the pancakes in batches. Cook until they're nicely browned on the bottom. Flip them and cook until the other side is likewise browned. Remove to a plate lined with paper towels, season to taste with salt and pepper, and serve immediately.

Cake and the Egg

THERE ARE MANY RECIPES ONLINE FOR eggless cakes, and surely you can rely entirely on chemical leaveners to create an airy crumb, and probably use a variety of modernist techniques to set a foam into a cakelike sponge. But cake could only have come to be because of eggs. Flour and liquid make dough; flour and egg make cake. Indeed, it's the most elementary of culinary creations and, given electric mixers, the easiest. Of course we almost always add sugar for sweetness. You can then flavor it any way you want, with vanilla, almond, or other extracts, or cocoa powder. You can enrich it with butter or, commonly, oil. And cheesecakes and certain chocolate cakes omit the flour entirely, relying only on egg, fat, and sugar. The egg is the single essential.

Here I'm going to focus on the basic cake, where the egg's primacy is unquestionable. But I also want to focus on cake for another reason: it's a preparation that has been replaced all but entirely in the home kitchen by a packaged mix. The processed food companies created the dump-and-stir cake early in the 1900s, and all you had to do was add water, since the mix included powdered eggs. But it didn't sell. Not long after World War II, when the food processing industry got into gear, the marketers figured out that they'd made it *too* easy. People wouldn't buy it if they didn't at least have the *illusion* of actually doing something on their own to create the cake. "Let's have them add eggs!" the marketers said. It worked. The life-giving eggs gave life to the boxed cake mix.

I say it's time to take back the cake. And I know all of you cooks who already love to make your own cakes will join me in encouraging others to bake a cake—yolks and sugar whipped to a foam, flour folded in, whites beaten to peaks and folded in, then baked.

That's all there is to it.

The "cake" part, anyway. Remember that a great cake is a composition; what makes it delicious is all the stuff you eat with it. A plate of boiled noodles is one thing; but boiled noodles tossed with egg yolk and bacon and Parmesan becomes a heavenly pasta carbonara. You could put two pieces of fried bread together and eat them and, well, consider how enticing that idea is. But: those two pieces of bread become something else if there's some great farmhouse cheddar melting between them. Add some ham? Yum. Use a Gruyère cheese instead, then put a fried egg on top with some Mornay sauce and you have a *croque madame*, a French classic that's out of this world.

Cake is no different from pasta or a slice of bread and should be thought of in exactly the same way. While your homemade sponge cake is going to taste delicious as is, when you add buttercream, lemon curd, and jam inside and cover it with a simple whipped cream concoction, you create an event.

I co-wrote the *Bouchon Bakery* cookbook, in which chef Sebastien Rouxel offers some astonishing cakes (and stresses the importance of the freezer, about which more below), but for this book I wanted to do some very basic cakes that can be used as launch points and make people feel comfortable with cakes, something I myself never really have. I'm a savory cook, more at home working the grill than the pastry station. So I brought in a ringer for one of the most important egg preparations in the entire egg pantheon, the cake, our great culinary symbol of celebration. I happen to have a talented wife, who happens to have a talented sister, Regina Simmons, who happens to be a professional baker in New York's Hudson Valley. Her forte is cake, specifically wedding cakes and other special-event cakes.

Regina agreed to fly to Cleveland and bake in my kitchen. What I like about Regina's techniques is that they are based on speed, resourcefulness, and economy. She's not lucky enough to have a fancy French oven, her mixer is twenty years old, and

sugar + eggs + flour = cake

she'll make do with any circular mold, dented cake pan, or wobbling cake ring she can find—hell, she could probably bake amazing cakes with a couple of hubcaps. It hardly matters because, as she says, "Cakes start out ugly, they all do. The fun is in making them beautiful."

The following are a few cake basics and three of Regina's signature cakes, as well as some creams and frostings. I'm not going to claim that these are not undertakings, but while they involve numerous steps, if you plan ahead and spread out the process over several days, they're all dead simple and absolutely delicious—and with just a little patience and practice, gorgeous as well. The coconut cake is probably the easiest, so if you're new to cakes, that's a good place to start.

THE KEYS TO FABULOUS CAKE

The importance of the freezer cannot be overstated. The first and perhaps most useful knowledge to have under your cap is how important it is to freeze cakes. They taste better after they've been frozen, their texture is improved, they're easier to work with and to frost or ice, and they cut more cleanly for a great presentation. Best of all, since these are often special-occasion creations, they can be made many days, even weeks, before you want to serve them. And they are very easy to transport when frozen, the perfect gift to bring to a friend. I've kept a well-wrapped cake in the freezer for more than two months without compromising it. You can make the sponge one weekend and freeze it, make the creams the next (they'll keep for a week in the fridge), and put the cake together at your leisure.

Parchment is your friend. By all means, bake in a springform pan if you wish. If you must have perfect edges, line only the bottom of your cake pan or use a proper cake ring. Regina lines whatever is at hand with parchment, sides and all, just smashes it down into the pan (making it stick to the sides with shortening or oil), not worrying about imperfections in the exterior of the cake—in fact, all those wrinkles and creases will just take in more tasty icing.

The icings/frostings/fillings are what make a cake truly delicious. Don't skimp on these, and consider using more than one in the same cake for more complex flavors, just as you would with any other dessert or any dish, period. These are also the most time-consuming elements in creating a great cake.

From a baking standpoint, the main thing to be is organized so that you get as much rise out of the sponge as possible. This means primarily two things: **prep your pans and preheat your oven before you start whipping your eggs.**

And one final note about pastry cream and buttercream: Here is where **it's important to know the salt level of whatever butter you use.** If you use unsalted butter, everything benefits from at least a pinch of salt, and anything chocolate benefits big-time from the right salt level. If you use salted butter, you often don't need to add extra salt to the creams.

Regina's Lemon Cream Cake

MAKES 1 LARGE CAKE, SERVES 20

This is one of Regina's most popular cakes, and I love it for the mixture of flavors. It's also relatively economical; while you have to make three different fillings, two others can be store-bought: jam and frozen fruit (which you pulverize). She makes a simple lemon curd, which becomes part of the layering and is also mixed into chantilly cream (whipped cream sweetened with confectioners' sugar); this lemon-chantilly is used to ice the finished cake and is also the main icing between the layers. The fat-rich buttercream prevents the fruit liquids from seeping into the cake itself.

The basic sponge can be used to make just about any kind of cake you wish, and is a standard biscuit, a French term designating that a meringue is folded into the base ingredients (yolks, sugar, flavoring), then baked.

Again, I'd like to stress that if you've got a lot going on in your life and don't have a half day to mosey in the kitchen, you should spread this process out over days or weeks, baking the sponge cakes first and freezing them, then making the three creams some other day. This way you can put it together when it's convenient and not feel harried.

1 recipe Basic Sponge Cake (page 116)

1 recipe Lemon Curd (page 118)

1 recipe Chantilly Cream (page 119)

1 recipe French Buttercream (page 120)

½ cup/150 grams raspberry jam

½ cup/120 grams frozen mixed berries that have been pulverized, while frozen, in a food processor

1 cup/100 grams cookie crumbs (any kind of plain butter or almond cookies or graham crackers, coarsely pulverized in a food processor), for decoration (optional)

A few sliced fresh strawberries, blackberries, or blueberries, for garnish

When you're ready to assemble and finish the cake, flip each sponge cake layer onto a cutting board, bottom side up. Using a serrated knife, cut the cake into two equal layers by beginning to slice horizontally into the side of the cake about an inch deep, then rotating the cake (or the board) counterclockwise (or clockwise if you're left-handed), continuing to slice in a circular motion toward the center until you are all the way through. This should give you two even layers without the aid of a jig. (I once cut through the top of one layer and Regina said, "Don't worry about it, you won't see it in the finished cake—the cream will hold it together." I love her easy, cavalier attitude.)

Ready a cake round (cut from heavy cardboard) slightly larger than the cake, or a large plate with no lip, or a cake platter, or a cutting board—really any flat surface that will allow you to move the cake as you ice it.

Combine two-thirds of the lemon curd with the chantilly cream and fold until combined. Place one of the bottom cake layers on your cake round, cut side up (if this is your first time, put down a sheet of parchment paper to make the cleanup easier). For each side of each layer (except the bottom), you're going to spread a thin coat of buttercream

first; this layer of fat prevents any berry juice from leaching into the cake. (For extra flavor and moisture, Regina sometimes first brushes the cake with a simple flavored syrup—sugar and water flavored with almond extract, for instance. Feel free to do this!) Next, spread a thin layer of lemon curd, 2 tablespoons or so, followed by a thin layer of jam, about 1 tablespoon or to taste.

Spoon out enough lemon-chantilly cream to create a ½-inch/1-centimeter layer and spread it evenly across the surface. Sprinkle half of the frozen berries on top.

The next layer will be one of the cake tops; before you place it on top of the frozen berries and cream, you need to prepare the underside as you did with the first coating of the sponge: spread a layer of buttercream, then lemon curd, then jam. Then flip it, coated-side down, onto the first frosted layer, sandwiching the lemon-chantilly between the two cake layers.

You should now be looking at the un-iced top of the second layer. Repeat the process with the following layers: buttercream, lemon curd, jam, chantilly cream, frozen berries. For the illustrations (page 111 and pages 113–15) we made a three-layer cake, but you could make one with four layers or as many as you wish.

When the layered cake has been constructed, an optional step is to coat the entire exterior with a thin layer of buttercream, called a crumb coat (not pictured). If you have time, chill the cake in the refrigerator so that the buttercream firms up; this will make icing the cake easier.

To ice the cake, use a cake spatula, or any long, flat-sided implement. Apply the lemon-chantilly cream to the sides, creating a ¾-inch/2-centimeter layer. Turn the board or plate toward you as you add the icing and smooth out the sides, holding the spatula still (a rotating cake stand or lazy Susan makes this very easy). When icing has been applied all around, continue to turn the plate to create a smooth surface. Don't worry about the top or bottom edges—you can give the bottom a coating of cookie crumbs and the top a decorative piping.

When the sides have been iced, apply a similar layer across the top. Again, spin the plate while holding the spatula still to achieve a perfectly smooth surface. If you don't have a long spatula, or have trouble creating a perfectly uniform top, feel free to make it wavy, or use the teeth of a serrated knife to make a decorative pattern. This can be done on the sides as well.

Now, as an optional but recommended step, make a cookie-crumb band around the cake by tilting the plate or board and pouring the crumbs around the base and halfway up the sides of the cake. Using a bench scraper or the flat side of a knife, press the crumbs gently into the icing so that they stick. Scrape away any excess crumbs for a clean appearance, or leave them for a more rustic appearance.

Put the remaining buttercream into a piping bag fitted with a large star tip (you can also use a sturdy plastic bag with a hole cut in one corner). Make a decorative border along the edges. In the illustrations, Regina is using a wave motion, down and up, down and up, as she circles the cake.

Pipe three small swirls in the center of the cake and garnish them with the fresh berries.

Freeze the cake, then wrap it and keep frozen until ready to serve or transport. Unwrap the cake when you remove it from the freezer and leave it out for an hour or two before serving, less if the weather or kitchen is particularly warm. Any leftovers can be wrapped carefully and frozen (or refrozen).

Mise en place (clockwise from mixer): lemon curd, heavy cream, pulverized
~~en~~ berries, raspberry jam, sponge cake, powdered sugar, and buttercream.

2. / Chantilly cream is simply whipping cream sweetened with confectioners'
sugar and often some kind of extract, here vanilla.

3. / Chantilly cream will be the main icing in this cake.

4. / It's further flavored with some lemon curd.

5. / Making the first layer, which is put together like all the rest:
a film of fatty buttercream first, which prevents liquids from leaching
into the sponge, followed by lemon curd.

6. / The layering of flavor continues with jam.

7. / The lemon-chantilly cream tops the jam.

8. / Pulverized frozen berries are the final element of the interior garnish. Never waste an opportunity to flavor cake.

11. / The top is coated.

12. / Holding the spatula still, rotate the cake to smooth the chantilly cream.

14. / Cookie crumbs add crunch, flavor, and color, and also conceal the bottom edge of the cake.

15. / Use a flat implement to press the cookie crumbs into the chantilly cream.

9. / *A sponge with jam, lemon curd, and buttercream tops the crushed berries.*

10. / *When all the layers have been completed, the cake is iced with the lemon-chantilly cream, sides first.*

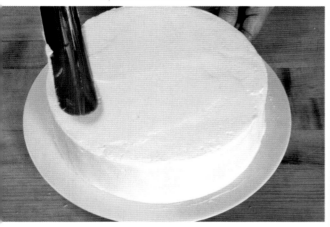

13. / *You'll be amazed how well rotating the cake works. It takes some practice and care, but a professional finish is within your reach.*

16. / *Piping the last of the buttercream through a large star tip around the outer edge of the cake.*

17. / *The finished cake, with multiple colors, textures, and flavors, is worthy of any kind of celebration.*

Basic Sponge Cake

MAKES 2 (8- OR 9-INCH) CAKE LAYERS

8 eggs, separated
2 cups/400 grams sugar
Pinch of salt
1½ cups/210 grams flour

Preheat the oven to 350°F/180°C. Grease the bottoms and sides of two 8- or 9-inch/20- or 23-centimeter cake pans or cake rings and line them with parchment. Set aside.

Put the yolks in a standing mixer fitted with a whisk attachment. (If you don't have a standing mixer, a hand blender with a whisk attachment or electric beaters will work, but they'll take a little more time. You can also use a big whisk, which, while requiring some effort, includes the advantage of burning off some of the calories you'll consume in the eating of this cake.) Turn the mixer on high and slowly add about two-thirds of the sugar, beating the yolks till they've doubled in volume and are light and fluffy, 3 to 5 minutes. (If you want to add flavorful extracts to your sponge, add them while mixing the yolks.) Pour them into a large mixing bowl.

Clean the whisk and bowl with soap and hot water, rinse thoroughly, dry, and return both to the mixer (errant yolk can prevent the whites from becoming a meringue). Add the whites and beat on high till they're frothy, then add the rest of the sugar slowly, about a tablespoon at a time, so that it has time to dissolve into the whites. Continue to beat the whites until all of the sugar is added and they form stiff peaks, 5 minutes or so depending on your mixer.

Add the salt to the flour and whisk thoroughly or, if it has been sitting for a long time, pulse it in a food processor or pass it through a sifter. Rain the flour over the egg yolks, using large sweeping circular motions with a wooden spoon to fold it in. When the flour is mostly incorporated, add one-quarter of the egg whites and fold these in the same way (fold slowly and gently to pop as few air bubbles in the egg whites as possible). Add the remaining egg whites in two additions and continue to fold until all of the ingredients are uniformly incorporated and you have a thick, just-pourable batter.

Divide the batter between the two lined pans, filling them two-thirds to three-quarters full. (If using 8-inch/20-centimeter pans, you'll have some batter left over. This can be piped or spooned onto a parchment-lined baking sheet and baked as you would cookies; to serve, dust with powdered sugar or glaze with chocolate—see page 130; these are sometimes referred to as Champagne cookies.)

Put the cakes in the oven immediately and bake until the centers are set, 20 to 30 minutes. You can use a cake tester or paring knife inserted into the center to judge doneness, but you can also simply tap the top of the cake; if it's not done, you will feel that the center is liquidy, like tapping a water bed. If you tap and the cake is clearly firm, it's done.

Remove the cakes from the oven and set them on a wire rack to cool completely. Lift them out of their molds and peel off the parchment paper. They can now be double-wrapped with plastic wrap and frozen. They can also be sliced and frozen, similarly wrapped, or they can be used right away.

1. / For a basic sponge cake, a cake pan or ring is lined with parchment, its edges trimmed for neatness.

2. / Egg yolks and sugar are foamed. Flour will be folded into this mixture.

3. / Last, the egg whites, whipped to stiff glossy peaks, are folded into the yolk-sugar-flour mixture.

4. / The batter is spread in the lined cake pan.

5. / The finished cake, removed from the pan.

6. / The cake can be sliced by rotating it at the same time that you gradually move a serrated knife through its center.

Lemon Curd

MAKES ABOUT 2½ CUPS/600 MILLILITERS

There are all kinds of ways of making lemon curd. Yolks only. Varying butter amounts. Whipping over a water bath. Even cooking it in a microwave. This is how Auntie Regina does it because, well, for a working mom of four with too much to do, this way works fast and is idiot-proof. (It is, of course, also delicious.) A little cornstarch helps to ensure that it sets up nicely so you don't need to worry about overcooking the eggs. You can also use this preparation for the Key Lime Tart (page 218) or any lemon tart—it's a dream.

1 cup/240 milliliters fresh lemon juice

1 tablespoon cornstarch

5 eggs

1 cup/200 grams sugar

½ cup/110 grams butter, cut into four or five pieces

Stir 2 tablespoons of the lemon juice into the cornstarch to make a slurry. Set aside.

Combine the eggs, the remaining lemon juice, and the sugar in a medium saucepan over medium-high heat (or high heat if you want it to go faster). Cook the mixture, whisking continuously, until it just starts to simmer and thicken. Add the lemon-cornstarch slurry and continue whisking until it thickens further and begins to simmer. Remove the pan from the heat and whisk in the butter, one chunk at a time. When the butter is melted, transfer the curd to a bowl and let it cool completely. Use right away or refrigerate for up to 5 days with plastic wrap pressed down onto its surface and a second layer of plastic covering the bowl.

Chantilly Cream

MAKES ABOUT 4 CUPS/1 LITER

This is a great all-purpose cream, as is or mixed with other ingredients.

2 cups/480 milliliters heavy whipping cream

½ to ⅔ cup/50 to 75 grams confectioners' sugar (depending on how sweet you want it)

Pinch of salt

1 tablespoon pure vanilla extract

Put the cream in the bowl of a standing mixer fitted with a whisk attachment and mix on high, sprinkling in the sugar as you do. Add the salt and vanilla and mix until incorporated and stiff peaks form. Refrigerate till chilled; this can be made up to 4 hours before using.

French Buttercream

MAKES ABOUT 4 CUPS/1 LITER

This is a simple buttercream, a cream whose consistency is dependent on the temperature you bring the sugar to, 235° to 240°F/113°C to 116°C, called the soft ball stage because when cool it will form a soft ball—that is, it will not have cooked to the point that it will harden when cooled. You'll need a candy thermometer for this. Regina stresses the importance of whipping the buttercream until it is room temperature so that the butter doesn't melt.

2 cups/400 grams sugar

½ cup/120 milliliters water

1 whole egg

3 egg yolks

2 cups/450 grams room-temperature butter, cut into 16 chunks

½ cup/225 grams vegetable shortening

2 teaspoons pure vanilla extract

Combine the sugar and water in a medium saucepan over high heat until the sugar has dissolved and begun to simmer. Lower the heat to medium and insert a candy thermometer; you'll need to keep an eye on the temperature while you whip the eggs.

Put the egg and yolks in the bowl of a standing mixer fitted with a whisk attachment and whip on high till the eggs have doubled in volume.

When the temperature of the sugar has exceeded 235°F/113°C (it can go as high as 240°F/116°C), pour it slowly into the eggs, with the mixer still running. Continue to whip the buttercream on high until the mixture is below 80°F/27°C, about 10 minutes (you can speed the cooling by holding a bag of ice against the mixing bowl). When the eggs and sugar have cooled, add the butter, a few chunks at a time, followed by the shortening and vanilla. Beat until all of the ingredients are incorporated. Use right away or cover with plastic wrap and refrigerate for up to a week, then allow it to come to room temperature before using.

1. / *Buttercream is nothing more than eggs, sugar (next photo), and butter.*

2. / *Eggs are whipped, and cooked sugar is added.*

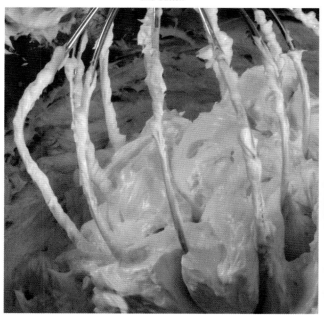

3. / *Fat is added after the sugar has cooled. Here we add a small amount of shortening for improved texture.*

4. / *Chocolate buttercream is simply buttercream with chocolate whipped in.*

COCONUT CREAM CAKE

1. / *The coconut cake is the most straightforward of the cakes here.*

2. / *Unlike our other layered cakes, this one uses a single icing for both the filling and covering the exterior. It's finished with a coating of coconut.*

Coconut Cream Cake

MAKES 1 LARGE CAKE, SERVES 20

This is a crowd pleaser and one of my son's new favorites—and one of mine, too, which is saying something because I've never really been a fan of coconut. What's great about this cake beyond the pleasure of eating it is that it's so easy to make, and to make pretty. It's supposed to be shaggy. And unlike the carpets of my 1970s Midwestern childhood, it won't go out of fashion.

This cake uses the same sponge recipe for the fancy-pants lemon cream cake(page 110), but we used all four layers, mainly because it gives you an excuse to eat more of the delicious coconut cream. Regina also uses the technique of painting each layer with coconut syrup (I'd gone with her to our local grocery store, where she spotted a can in the cocktail mixers section—any decent coconut syrup will do). This adds flavor and moisture to the sponge.

The sponge can be made a week ahead and frozen. The creams can be made up to 2 days before completing the cake.

1 recipe Basic Sponge Cake (page 116)

1 recipe Chantilly Cream (page 119)

1 recipe Vanilla Pastry Cream (page 125)

3 cups sweetened shredded coconut

½ cup/120 milliliters coconut syrup

When you're ready to assemble and finish the cake, flip each sponge cake layer onto a cutting board, bottom side up. Using a serrated knife, cut the cake into two equal layers by beginning to slice horizontally into the side of the cake about an inch deep, then rotating the cake (or the board) counterclockwise (or clockwise if you're left-handed), continuing to slice in a circular motion toward the center until you are all the way through. This should give you two even layers.

Ready a cake round (cut from heavy cardboard) slightly larger than the cake, or a large plate with no lip, or a cake platter, or a cutting board—really any flat surface that will allow you to move the cake as you ice it.

Combine the chantilly cream and pastry cream and fold to mix. Add 1 cup of the shredded coconut and fold till everything is uniformly combined.

Place one of the bottom cake layers on the cake round, cut side up, and brush it with coconut syrup, then spread it with about ½ inch/1.25 centimeters of the coconut-laced cream. Brush the underside of one of the top cake layers with coconut syrup and place it on top of the layer of coconut cream. Repeat this process with the remaining two layers. Brush the top and sides of the cake with more coconut syrup, if you have any left.

Spread the remaining coconut cream evenly along the sides and then across the top of the cake, smoothing all surfaces. Coat the entire cake with the remaining shredded coconut. Press the coconut gently into the cream with a bench scraper or flat side of a knife so that it adheres. Serve right away, or refrigerate or freeze.

1. / *Vanilla pastry cream* mise en place: *dairy, yolks, sugar, butter, milk thickened with cornstarch.*

2. / *Hot milk and cream are added to the yolks and sugar to temper the eggs; then, top right, the egg mixture is returned to the pan.*

3. / *The pastry cream, once it has cooked and thickened, is passed through a strainer to filter out any egg that may have coagulated.*

4. / *The pastry cream sets up as it cools.*

Vanilla Pastry Cream

MAKES ABOUT 2½ CUPS/600 MILLILITERS

As noted on page 171, pastry cream is simply crème anglaise thickened with either flour or cornstarch. I prefer cornstarch because it's quicker and easier and there's no difference in texture or flavor. Regina's pastry cream is a little lighter than mine; for the Coconut Cream Cake (page 123), we used her superb version.

2 tablespoons cornstarch

1½ cups/360 milliliters milk

½ cup/120 milliliters heavy cream

2 egg yolks

½ packed cup/100 grams light brown sugar

Pinch of salt

¼ cup/60 grams butter, at room temperature, cut into 2 pieces

1 tablespoon pure vanilla extract

Mix the cornstarch with about 3 tablespoons of the milk to make a slurry and set aside.

Combine the remaining milk and the cream in a small saucepan and bring to a simmer over high heat—be careful not to let it boil.

Whisk the yolks with the sugar and salt in a bowl until the mixture is creamy.

When the milk-cream has come to a simmer, reduce the heat to medium and pour half of it into the egg-sugar mixture, whisking continuously. Put the pan back on the heat and pour the egg mixture into it. Whisk just until it comes up to a simmer, then add the cornstarch slurry (stir it first if the starch has sunk to the bottom). When the sauce comes back up to heat and has thickened, remove it from the heat. Whisk in the butter and vanilla and strain into a clean bowl. Cover and refrigerate until completely chilled; this will keep for several days.

Chocolate Mocha Cake

MAKES 1 LARGE CAKE, SERVES 20

There's no mystery to chocolate cake—it's simply sponge cake with chocolate, usually cocoa powder. And it's a great cake to have in your repertoire. This recipe will work with regular old inexpensive cocoa, but if you're going to go to the effort, I urge you to use the best you can find. I was introduced to Guittard Cocoa Rouge, which is especially well suited to baking. Be aware that if you're using alkalized (usually labeled "Dutch process") cocoa powder, it won't interact with baking soda, which reacts to acid. We use three flavoring devices here: a basic all-purpose chocolate glaze, a mocha pastry cream (flavored with espresso powder), and chocolate buttercream for decoration.

1 recipe Chocolate Sponge Cake (page 128)

½ recipe Chantilly Cream (page 119)

1 recipe Mocha Pastry Cream (page 128)

1 recipe Chocolate Buttercream (page 129)

1 recipe Chocolate Glaze (page 130)

Cocoa powder, for garnish

When you're ready to assemble and finish the cake, flip each sponge cake layer onto a cutting board, bottom side up. Using a serrated knife, cut the cake into two equal layers by beginning to slice horizontally into the side of the cake about an inch deep, then rotating the cake (or the board) counterclockwise (or clockwise if you're left-handed), continuing to slice in a circular motion toward the center until you are all the way through. This should give you two even layers.

Ready a cake round (cut from heavy cardboard) slightly larger than the cake, or a large plate with no lip, a cake platter, or a cutting board—really any flat surface that will allow you to move the cake as you ice it.

Fold together the chantilly cream and half of the mocha pastry cream till they're uniformly mixed.

Place one of the bottom cake layers on the cake round, cut side up. Spread a thin layer of chocolate buttercream on top, then a layer of plain mocha pastry cream, followed by a layer of mocha-chantilly cream. Spread a layer of chocolate buttercream on the underside of one of the top cake layers and place it on top of the mocha-chantilly cream. Repeat with the remaining layers.

Warm the chocolate glaze in the microwave in increments, stirring to make it uniformly warm and pourable. Pour it over the top of the cake, all the way to the edges.

Ice the sides of the cake with the remaining mocha-chantilly cream.

Put the remaining buttercream into a piping bag fitted with a large star tip (or a sturdy plastic bag with a hole cut in one corner). Pipe decorative florets around the edges of the cake and dust them by sifting cocoa powder over them.

This cake can be frozen and wrapped until you're ready to cut and serve it.

When serving a large cake to a big group, don't limit yourself to cutting wedges—squares are perfectly fine.

Chocolate Sponge Cake

MAKES 2 (8- OR 9-INCH) CAKE LAYERS

1¾ cups/245 grams flour

¾ cup/75 grams unsweetened cocoa powder

1½ teaspoons baking powder

1½ teaspoons baking soda

2 eggs

2 cups/400 grams sugar

½ teaspoon salt

1 cup/240 milliliters hot coffee

1 cup/240 milliliters milk

½ cup/120 milliliters vegetable oil

2 teaspoons pure vanilla extract

Preheat the oven to 350°F/180°C. Grease the bottoms and sides of two 8- or 9-inch/20- or 23-centimeter cake pans or rings and line them with parchment paper.

Sift the flour, cocoa, baking powder, and baking soda into a medium bowl.

Combine the eggs, sugar, and salt in the bowl of a standing mixer fitted with a whisk attachment and whip on high till the eggs are creamy, a minute or two.

Add the flour-cocoa mixture and mix on high till combined. Add the remaining ingredients and continue to mix on high for another 2 minutes or so.

Pour the batter into the prepared pans or rings and bake till set in the middle, 20 to 25 minutes.

Remove the cakes from the oven and set them on a wire rack to cool completely. Lift them out of their molds and peel off the parchment paper. They can now be double-wrapped with plastic wrap and frozen. They can also be sliced and frozen, similarly wrapped. Or they can be used right away.

Mocha Pastry Cream

MAKES ABOUT 3 CUPS/720 MILLILITERS

This is best made a day or two before you need it so that it's thoroughly chilled.

3 tablespoons cornstarch

1½ cups/360 milliliters milk

½ cup/120 milliliters heavy cream

4 egg yolks

½ packed cup/100 grams light brown sugar

½ teaspoon salt

¼ cup/25 grams unsweetened cocoa powder

2 tablespoons instant espresso powder

¼ cup/60 grams butter, at room temperature, cut into 2 pieces

1 tablespoon pure vanilla extract

Mix the cornstarch with about 3 tablespoons of the milk to make a slurry and set aside.

Combine the remaining milk and the cream in a small saucepan and bring to a simmer over high heat—be careful not to let it boil.

Whisk the yolks with the sugar and salt in a bowl until the mixture is creamy.

When the milk-cream has come to a simmer, reduce the heat to medium and pour half of it into the egg-sugar mixture, whisking continuously. Put the pan back on the heat and pour the egg mixture into it. Whisk in the cocoa and espresso powders and continue to whisk just until it comes up to a simmer, then add the cornstarch slurry (stir it first if the starch has sunk to the bottom). When the mixture comes back up to a simmer and has thickened, remove it from the heat. Whisk in the butter and vanilla and strain into a clean bowl. Cover and refrigerate until it is completely chilled; this can be made several days before using.

Chocolate Buttercream

MAKES ABOUT 2½ CUPS/600 MILLILITERS

This rich, all-purpose buttercream can be used as an icing itself; here it's used for filling and decorating the chocolate mocha cake.

1 cup/200 grams sugar

¼ cup/60 milliliters water

3 egg yolks

1 whole egg

1 cup/225 grams butter, cut into about 15 pieces and brought to room temperature

2 teaspoons pure vanilla extract

1 cup/200 grams semisweet or bittersweet chocolate chips or chopped chocolate, melted and slightly cooled

In a small saucepan, combine the sugar and water over high heat. Bring to a boil and cook for 3 to 5 minutes. (The sugar syrup should register between 235° and 240°F/113° and 116°C on a candy thermometer.)

While the sugar syrup cooks, combine the egg yolks and whole egg in the bowl of a standing mixer fitted with the whisk attachment. Whip the eggs on high speed until tripled in volume. This will take about as long as needed to cook the sugar syrup.

With the mixer still running, pour the sugar syrup slowly into the beaten eggs. Continue to whip until the outside of the bowl has cooled, 8 to 10 minutes. Reduce the speed to medium and add a piece of the butter. After it begins to become incorporated, add the remaining butter, one piece at a time. The butter may look as if it's breaking, but keep whipping it, and the mixture will come together.

When all of the butter is incorporated, add the vanilla and chocolate, return the speed to high, and beat until the cream becomes smooth and luscious. Use right away or refrigerate till needed (and allow to warm till it's pliable before using).

Chocolate Glaze

MAKES ABOUT 2½ CUPS/600 MILLILITERS

Regina adapted this easy all-purpose chocolate glaze from a recipe by Dolores Casella. It is a liquid when heated, but sets up soft and firm at room temperature. We drizzle it on coconut cookies, pour it over ice cream, and use it for the glossy top of Regina's Chocolate Mocha Cake (page 126).

½ cup/120 milliliters evaporated milk

½ cup/100 grams sugar

Pinch of salt

1 cup/200 grams semisweet chocolate chips

¼ cup/60 grams butter, cut into pieces

2 tablespoons pure maple syrup or corn syrup

2 teaspoons pure vanilla extract

Combine the evaporated milk, sugar, and salt in a medium saucepan over medium-high heat. Rub a little butter around the inner rim of the pan to help prevent the milk from boiling over. Bring the mixture to a simmer, reduce the heat to medium-low, and cook for 5 minutes. Remove the pot from the heat and whisk in half of the chocolate. When it begins to melt, add the rest of the chocolate, followed by the butter, syrup, and vanilla. Whisk until all of the ingredients are incorporated.

Pour the mixture into a clean bowl to cool. When ready to use, microwave until it's pourable, about 30 seconds (take it out midway and stir it).

1. / Mise en place *for a simple all-purpose glaze: evaporated milk, butter, sugar, and chocolate, with additional flavorings of maple syrup and vanilla.*

2. / *The evaporated milk and sugar are simmered for 5 minutes. Then the pan is removed from the heat, and the chocolate and other ingredients are stirred in.*

3. / *The finished chocolate glaze.*

Rum-Soaked Cherry Bread (or Muffins) with Almond-Sugar Topping

MAKES 12 MUFFINS OR 1 STANDARD LOAF

I'm including a quick bread to show how easy they are when you know the ratio. The basic quick bread (or muffin) ratio is two parts each flour and liquid, one part each eggs and butter. If they're sweet, and most are, you can add sugar, up to the amount of the eggs by weight. Here I'm simply making a sweet quick bread flavored with almond and garnished with cherries, with the addition of browned butter and an almond topping, but really you can take this basic ratio—equal parts flour and milk, half as much egg and butter—in any direction you wish. If you have a scale, weigh your eggs first and adjust accordingly, then place your mixing bowl on the scale and pour the ingredients directly in (no need for measuring cups). This is the neatest and most reliable way to mix and bake.

Toppings are not required, but they do add flavor, texture, and sweetness. This streusel topping, which I learned from Sebastien Rouxel while working on the Bouchon Bakery *cookbook, is basically equal parts all-purpose flour, almond flour (also known as almond meal), sugar, and butter. But you can also change the topping to something more like a crumble, with equal parts brown sugar, flour, oats, and butter, or simply use chopped nuts. Chef Rouxel also likes his batters to rest overnight to give the batter time to hydrate for a better interior crumb, but you can omit this step if you're pressed for time. Pastry chef and instructor Cory Barrett was the first to teach me to flour berries or other fruit before adding them to a batter; this will prevent them from sinking to the bottom.*

FOR THE STREUSEL TOPPING:

½ cup/70 grams all-purpose flour

½ cup/70 grams almond flour (almond meal)

⅓ cup/70 grams sugar

3½ tablespoons/50 grams butter, chilled and diced

FOR THE BATTER:

3 eggs

1 cup/240 milliliters milk

2 cups/280 grams all-purpose flour, plus more for dusting the cherries

½ cup/100 grams sugar

½ cup/110 grams butter

1 teaspoon pure almond extract

1 teaspoon pure vanilla extract

2 teaspoons baking powder

½ cup/55 grams dried tart cherries, soaked for at least 8 hours in light rum

Combine all of the topping ingredients as if making a pie dough; pinch the butter until it is in tiny chunks. Cover and refrigerate till ready to use.

For the cake, mix the eggs, milk, flour, and sugar in a large mixing bowl. Whisk just till combined.

Melt the butter in a small saucepan over medium-high heat. When the crackling sound subsides and all that's visible is froth, the water has cooked out and the butter will begin to brown. When it has a nutty aroma, pour it immediately into the batter, whisking continuously until the batter is smooth and uniform. Add the extracts and whisk to incorporate.

Cover and refrigerate for 8 to 24 hours if possible.

Preheat the oven to 350°F/180°C. Butter a standard loaf pan or 12-cup standard muffin tin or coat it with nonstick baking spray.

Whisk the baking powder into the chilled batter. Put about ½ cup flour in a plastic bag. Drain the cherries (save the cherry-flavored rum for a cocktail!). Add the cherries to the flour and shake to coat, then strain out the excess flour through a basket strainer.

Fold the cherries into the batter. Pour the batter into the prepared loaf pan or muffin cups. Top with the streusel mixture. Bake until a paring knife inserted in the center comes out clean, about 40 minutes for muffins, 1 hour for a loaf.

Emilia's Carrot Cake

MAKES 1 LOAF OR 12 CUPCAKES

Don't let the long list of ingredients (mainly spices) frighten you. This is still a quick bread, a simple cake anchored by flour and egg. It's also virtually an American tradition, especially with the cream cheese icing.

FOR THE CAKE:

¼ cup/60 milliliters dark rum

⅓ cup/55 grams raisins

1⅓ cups/185 grams flour

1¼ teaspoons baking powder

1 teaspoon baking soda

1 teaspoon salt

2 teaspoons ground cinnamon

½ teaspoon ground allspice

½ teaspoon ground nutmeg

½ teaspoon ground cardamom

½ teaspoon ground ginger

3 eggs

1 teaspoon pure vanilla extract

1 cup/200 grams granulated sugar

¾ cup/180 milliliters vegetable oil

⅓ cup/60 grams applesauce

8 ounces/225 grams peeled, grated carrots (about 5 large carrots)

½ cup/50 grams chopped walnuts (optional)

FOR THE CREAM CHEESE FROSTING:

8 ounces/225 grams cream cheese, at room temperature

1½ cups/150 grams confectioners' sugar

¼ cup/60 grams butter, at room temperature

1 teaspoon fresh lemon juice

First, make the cake. In a small saucepan, combine the rum and the raisins and bring to a boil over medium-high heat. Remove the pan from the heat, and set aside to steep.

Preheat the oven to 350°F/180°C. Butter a standard loaf pan or coat it with nonstick baking spray.

In a medium bowl, combine the flour, baking powder, baking soda, salt, and spices.

In another medium bowl, whisk together the eggs and vanilla until well combined. Then whisk in the sugar and beat until incorporated. Next, whisk in the oil, followed by the applesauce. You should have a homogeneous yellow batter.

Now slowly begin to rain the dry ingredients into the batter. Whisk just until the flour is absorbed. Do not overwork the batter.

Squeeze out any excess liquid from the carrots and fold them into the batter. Next, fold in the walnuts (if using) and the raisins, along with any rum that may be left in the saucepan.

Pour the batter into the prepared loaf pan and bake until a toothpick inserted into the center of the loaf comes out clean, about 1 hour (check after 50 minutes).

Remove from the oven and allow to cool.

While the loaf is cooling, combine all of the frosting ingredients in a medium bowl and mash and whip until everything is incorporated. You can also use a standing mixer with a paddle attachment, but if the ingredients are not chilled, a whisk results in the best texture.

Turn the cooled loaf out of the pan and top with the cream cheese frosting.

Make-Ahead Brownies

MAKES 24 (3-INCH/7.5-CENTIMETER) SQUARE BROWNIES

I used to make brownies in a 9-by-13-inch/23-by-33-centimeter baking dish, but they disappeared too quickly. Not anymore. Now I make a big batch of these fudgy, delicious brownies, to freeze and have on hand whenever the urge strikes. My sister-in-law and baking maven, Regina, makes these brownies routinely because they sell out where she bakes, Verdigris, in the lovely town of Hudson, New York. I love taking practices common to the professional kitchen and introducing them to the home, where they are especially useful.

As a kid, when I got my hands on a fabulous brownie and found it packed with walnuts, I felt cheated. Why, I wondered, did someone ruin a perfectly good brownie by putting nuts in it? But if you're a nut lover, feel free to add 1½ cups/130 grams chopped walnuts at the end. If not, and you want even more chocolate, add more chocolate chips! (One caveat: If you're like me, you're going to be eating these while they're still frozen; they're excellent this way, but the chips are particularly crunchy, so omit the chips if you intend to serve them frozen. That said, what a brilliant idea, putting chocolate chips into fudgy brownies! Regina uses the Ghirardelli brand, which is widely available and good quality.)

These are as easy to make as pancakes: combine the dry ingredients, combine the wet ingredients, stir, and pour. If you don't have what is known in the industry as a half sheet pan (13 by 18 inches/33 by 46 centimeters), halve the recipe or use an 11-by-15-inch/28-by-38-centimeter jelly roll pan. The 1-inch depth results in a fudgy, dense texture.

2 cups/280 grams flour

2 cups/200 grams unsweetened cocoa powder

2 teaspoons baking powder

1 teaspoon salt

8 eggs

4 cups/400 grams sugar

4 teaspoons pure vanilla extract

1 pound/450 grams butter, melted

2 cups/340 grams semisweet chocolate chips

Preheat the oven to 350°F/180°C. Line a half sheet pan or jelly roll pan with parchment paper and set aside.

Sift together the flour, cocoa, and baking powder in a large mixing bowl, and add the salt.

In another large mixing bowl, combine the eggs, sugar, and vanilla and whisk till well creamed, then pour in the melted butter in a thin stream, whisking continuously.

Combine the wet and the dry ingredients and stir or whisk to incorporate. Stir in the chocolate chips.

Pour the batter into the parchment-lined pan and bake until just set, 20 to 25 minutes.

Cool, turn out onto a cutting board, and cut the brownies to the desired size. Wrap each brownie individually in plastic and store in the freezer (but you'd better eat one or two right away just to make sure they're good).

1. / *Making brownies like the pros, in a baking sheet tray.*

2. / *Line the sheet tray with parchment to make the brownies easy to remove.*

3. / *Mark your lines before cutting.*

4. / *It helps to have a long knife, but a pizza cutter will also work well here.*

5. / *Cut into squares.*

6. / *Wrapped individually in plastic and frozen, the brownies keep for months, a great snack and a worthy dessert for impromptu dinner parties.*

Pancakes

MAKES ABOUT 8 (6-INCH/15-CENTIMETER) PANCAKES

Pancakes are so easy and delicious when made from scratch, especially if you have a scale. Whenever I see a pancake "mix" in a cute little cloth sack for $7.99 I want to pull my hair out. If your kitchen is well organized, with all of the ingredients you use on a regular basis in one place, it should be one quick step to gather the dry ingredients (flour, sugar, baking powder, salt), and another 15 seconds to set out the wet ingredients (milk, eggs, butter, vanilla). Combine the wet, combine the dry, add the dry to the wet, and stir (the less the better). You can do this faster than it takes your pan or griddle to get hot.

I love pancakes for their simplicity, of course, but they are an extraordinary window into the power of the egg. Without eggs, you wouldn't want to eat them. With eggs, they are one of the great staples of the American kitchen.

1 cup/240 milliliters milk

2 eggs

¼ cup/60 grams butter, melted

1 teaspoon pure vanilla extract

1⅓ to 1½ cups/200 grams flour

2 tablespoons sugar

2 teaspoons baking powder

½ teaspoon salt

Combine the milk, eggs, butter, and vanilla in a large bowl and whisk well till they're thoroughly combined.

In a medium bowl, combine the flour, sugar, baking powder (pressed through a strainer if it's pebbly), and salt.

Pour the dry ingredients into the wet mixture and whisk or stir till the batter is smooth. This ratio results in a fairly thick batter, and thick, cakey pancakes. If you like them thinner, add a little more milk.

Cook on a lightly oiled griddle or pan over medium heat until done, a few minutes per side.

Corn and Sweet Pepper Fritters
with Chipotle-Lime Mayonnaise

MAKES ABOUT 25 FRITTERS

I love fritters in part because the ease of making them is so disproportionate to their deliciousness. Surely something so delicious and special shouldn't be so easy to make! But when you realize that fritter batter is simply pancake batter without the butter and sugar, then you can see not only why they're so easy but how infinitely variable they are. Pour the batter over any tender sweet vegetable and you have a great fritter. I've done all kinds of fritters—curried pea, salt cod, zucchini, apple, you name it. Choose your favorites and you can't go wrong. Here, it's corn, sweet pepper, and onion, dipped in a lime-chipotle mayonnaise, a flavor combination I return to again and again.

FOR THE BATTER:

1 cup/140 grams flour

1 teaspoon baking powder

1 teaspoon ground cumin

½ teaspoon ground coriander

½ teaspoon salt

½ teaspoon freshly ground black pepper

½ cup/120 milliliters milk (or water or stock)

1 egg

FOR THE DIPPING SAUCE:

¾ cup/180 milliliters mayonnaise

1 chipotle pepper in adobo sauce, seeded and minced

1 tablespoon fresh lime juice

Cayenne pepper (optional)

FOR THE FRITTERS:

1 cup/170 grams corn kernels (preferably fresh, but thawed frozen will work)

1 cup/130 grams diced red bell pepper

½ cup/50 grams small-diced sweet onion

¼ cup/7 grams minced fresh cilantro

Vegetable oil for pan-frying

Stir together all of the batter ingredients in a small bowl. Set aside.

Stir together all of the dipping sauce ingredients, taste, and adjust the seasonings as you wish— you may want to add more lime juice or cayenne. Set aside.

For the fritters, combine the corn, bell pepper, onion, and cilantro in a medium bowl and stir till the ingredients are uniformly dispersed. Pour just enough batter over the mixture to coat and hold them together (you may not need all the batter) and stir.

Preheat the oven to 200°F/95°C. Line a plate with paper towels.

Pour ½ inch/1 centimeter oil into a skillet over high heat. When the oil is hot (350°F/180°C) drop tablespoonfuls of the vegetable-batter mixture into the oil (as the temperature of the oil comes back up, you may need to reduce the heat to medium-high). Cook the fritters for a few minutes on each side, turning them as necessary for even browning.

Remove a fritter and cut it in half. If it's cooked through (the batter is not runny inside), remove all of the fritters to the paper towel–lined plate. Keep these in the oven while you make successive batches.

Serve hot, with the dipping sauce.

1. / *Fritters are nothing more than tasty ingredients bound with what amounts to pancake batter and then fried.*

2. / *Use only as much batter as you need to bind the ingredients; the batter will puff and expand.*

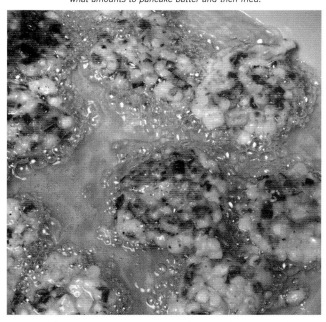

3. / *These employ the pan-fry technique, with just enough oil in the pan to come halfway up the sides of the fritters (though they could be deep-fried as well).*

4. / *This cross section shows a perfect dispersion of vegetable within the right amount of batter, a sight that never fails to make me lust for fritters.*

Shrimp Tempura with Tentsuyu Dipping Sauce

SERVES 4 AS A FIRST COURSE

In the United States most tempura batter seems to be a mixture of low-protein flour and non-gluten starch for simple crispness. But in fact, when tempura traveled from Portugal to Japan (via missionaries in the sixteenth century), Japan elevated it to great heights, with the addition of a whole egg. The egg adds flavor, but if you're not careful, it can result in a soft rather than crisp batter.

One of my recipe testers, Matt Kayahara, is interested in Japanese cuisine (he's one-quarter Japanese himself), so I asked him to create this entire recipe—not just the batter but the dashi (an elegant but very easy stock made of seaweed and bonito flakes) for the traditional dipping sauce called tentsuyu. *Matt says that soft water is a must for the dashi, so if you live in an area with hard water (water with more than 60 ppm calcium carbonate), use bottled water. He also notes that the dashi is very volatile and should be made the day of (it's quick and easy, so this shouldn't be a problem). You'll have a little more than you need; stir in a couple tablespoons of miso paste for a refreshing soup to accompany the shrimp.*

We found that the steam from cooked vegetables softened the fried batter too much, so we went with shrimp instead. The key is to mix the batter just before frying, but barely stirring it so that you develop as little gluten as possible and so that you have little clumps of dry flour floating in the batter (this helps to ensure maximum crispness, as does using low-gluten cake flour). For even more crispness, some chefs sprinkle a little extra batter over the shrimp after it's in the oil.

FOR THE DASHI:

1 quart/1 liter water (see headnote)

½ ounce/15 grams kombu (four small sheets or one large sheet)

1 ounce/25 grams bonito flakes (about 1 cup)

FOR THE DIPPING SAUCE:

½ cup/120 milliliters soy sauce, preferably Japanese

½ cup/120 milliliters mirin

2 to 3 tablespoons/60 to 90 milliliters rice-wine vinegar

¼ cup/60 grams grated daikon, drained of excess liquid

1 tablespoon grated fresh ginger, drained of excess liquid

FOR THE TEMPURA:

16 large shrimp (about 1 pound/450 grams), tails on, peeled and deveined

Vegetable oil for deep-frying

½ cup/70 grams cake flour

2 tablespoons/15 grams cornstarch

1 egg, beaten

Ice-cold water, enough to bring the volume of the egg to 150 milliliters

To make the dashi, put the water and kombu in a medium pot over high heat, bring to 140°F/60°C, and reduce the heat to maintain this temperature for 1 hour. Remove the kombu and raise the temperature to 175°F/80°C. Add the bonito flakes, steep for about 20 seconds, then strain through a coffee filter set in a mesh strainer.

To make the dipping sauce, combine 2 cups/480 milliliters of the dashi with the soy sauce, mirin, and vinegar in a small saucepan over medium heat. Bring to a simmer, then remove the pan from the heat and add the daikon and ginger. Cover and set aside.

To prevent the shrimp from curling tightly as they fry, squeeze them and press them down on a cutting board till you feel their shape give way and they flop limply when held by the tail.

In a large pot with high sides, heat 3 inches/ 7.5 centimeters oil to 350°F/180°C. Line a plate with paper towels and set aside.

When the oil is hot, whisk the flour and cornstarch together. In a separate bowl, beat the egg and water together, then add it to the flour mixture and whisk or stir gently with chopsticks until a lumpy batter forms. Dip the shrimp in the batter and deep-fry until brown and crisp and cooked through, 2 to 3 minutes. Drain them briefly on the paper towel–lined plate and serve immediately with the dipping sauce.

Popovers with Raspberry Jam and Powdered Sugar

MAKES 2 LARGE OR 4 MINI POPOVERS

This is another miraculous egg-dependent dish. It's very similar to the gougère *and profiterole, though it doesn't contain fat; rather it is cooked in fat. Because there is no fat to prevent gluten from forming, popovers are chewier and breadier than profiteroles. And yet the mechanics are similar—the steam releasing within the batter, the egg protein containing the steam and allowing them to puff. Indeed, they can puff even more than* gougères *because the gluten makes the flour elastic, so the inside remains delicate and custardy while the exterior browns.*

Because the steam remains trapped inside, the popover will contract as it cools, causing the lovely popover towers to fall, so they should be served straight from the oven. If they're going to sit for several minutes before being served, it's a good idea to remove them from the oven 5 minutes before they're done, pierce each one straight down through the center with a paring knife, and return them to the oven; this allows steam to escape while the heat solidifies the interior structure.

Popovers are a weekend treat, served with jam and powdered sugar. Make the batter before you go to bed, cover it, and let it sit out on the counter so that the flour is fully hydrated in the morning when you go to cook them. They get the most lift when cooked in a popover or mini popover pan (I prefer the latter), but you can use any kind of mold.

1 cup/240 milliliters milk

2 eggs

1 scant cup/130 grams flour

½ teaspoon salt (if using unsalted butter)

¼ cup/60 grams butter, melted

Raspberry jam, for serving

Confectioners' sugar, for serving

Combine the milk, eggs, flour, and salt (if using) in a medium bowl and whisk till thoroughly combined. Cover and allow to rest for at least 1 hour or up to 12 hours.

Preheat the oven to 450°F/230°C (or 425°F/220°C if your oven will smoke at 450°F/230°C) and put a popover pan in the oven. When you're ready to cook the popovers, remove the pan and divide the melted butter among the cups you're using. Pour the batter into each cup, about three-quarters full. Bake for 10 minutes, reduce the oven temperature to 375°F/190°C, and continue baking for 25 to 30 minutes. Try one—they should be solid but creamy in the center.

Dust the popovers with confectioners' sugar and serve immediately, with jam on the side.

Crêpes

MAKES 8 TO 10 CRÊPES

The crêpe, featuring the thinnest of our egg batters, is one of the many underused preparations in the home kitchen. At the most liquidy end of the dough-batter continuum, the crêpe is a pancake made possible by the miraculous egg. Crêpes are simple to make, and I like to use them as a tool to turn leftovers into a new and fresh meal. This is a recipe to use when you have, say, some leftover Blanquette de Veau (page 156) or Chicken Fricassee (page 159). Or, if you have a hankering for creamy morels but don't want to make an omelet (page 61), crêpes are perfect packages for the mushrooms—simply add chives or other herbs to the crêpe batter and use stock as the liquid. If you want a quick sweet dessert, instructions for crêpes suzette follow the basic recipe here. For a cold preparation, fill them with pastry cream. They can also be made ahead and reheated.

It's a simple ratio: two parts each liquid and egg to one part flour by weight. So if you just wanted a couple of crêpes for yourself, you could weigh 1 egg and stir in the same weight of liquid and half as much flour. One egg yields two 8-inch/20-centimeter crêpes.

4 eggs
1 cup/240 milliliters milk, water, or stock
Pinch of salt
1 scant cup/130 grams flour

Combine the ingredients and stir or whisk until the mixture is uniform. Let the batter rest for at least 15 minutes or up to several hours.

Heat a pan over medium-low heat (use a pan with an 8-inch/20-centimeter surface, preferably nonstick; of course, if you own a crêpe pan, use that). Wipe the pan with a little oil or butter and pour in a little less than ½ cup batter, just enough to coat the bottom.

You can either let the crêpe cook through without flipping it or flip the crêpe to cook both sides. If you'd like some browning on the crêpe, cook it over medium heat. The whole thing will take just a minute or so.

To serve the crêpe, spoon your desired filling down the center, fold the crêpe over it, and garnish with fresh herbs.

To make crêpes suzette:

¼ cup/60 grams butter

¼ cup/50 grams sugar

¼ cup/60 milliliters fresh orange juice

Zest of 1 orange

8 to 10 crêpes

⅓ cup/75 milliliters Grand Marnier
or other orange liqueur

Combine the butter, sugar, and orange juice and zest in a medium sauté pan. Bring the mixture to a simmer over medium-high heat and then reduce the heat to low. Reheat the crêpes in the liquid, one by one, folding them in half and then in half again into a quarter circle. Keep each one on the side of the sauté pan. When they are all hot and folded, arrange them overlapping in the pan, pull the pan off the heat, and add the Grand Marnier (off the burner because, while not likely, the fumes can ignite as you pour, which could then detonate the bottle). Return the heat to medium-high and ignite the liqueur by tilting the pan toward the gas flame, or ignite the alcohol fumes with a match or lighter.

Serve immediately.

Part Five

Egg / Separated

The Yolk

So we come now to consider the white and the yolk, not divorced, because they will always be one and are always best that way, but, for now, separated.

The white is the man of the house, Mr. Protein, transparent, guileless, extremely useful, but bland and straightforward. The yolk is the woman, voluptuous, manipulative, brilliant, rich, nutritious, seductive, the center of life. That's one guy's view of the egg, anyhow.

The yolk is my favorite part of the egg. It is a wondrous substance for all the reasons noted above. And in a custard, the difference is revealing. A custard made from whole egg is smooth and silky if prepared correctly, but firm, with something close to a bite. A custard made with egg yolk alone, on the other hand, is deeply creamy and satisfying. You couldn't slice it cleanly, nor should you want to. It's meant to be scooped, soft and ethereal on the tongue.

And because it's soft, it's always best paired with something crisp, crunchy, shattering. This is why the crème brûlée is perhaps the perfect dessert, not just for its simplicity but for its capacity, given the bittersweet brittle surface and creamy depths, to satisfy our childish love of comfort and smoothness and sweets, as well as our adult appreciation for contrast and refinement.

For those who love the craft of cooking, the yolk is an extraordinary tool, capable of turning vegetable oil into a semisolid and extraordinary condiment, butter into a rapturous sauce, and cream into an unparalleled emollient at the table.

• • •

Egg / Separated / Yolk / Raw —————

Garnish

HOME COOKS TEND TO THINK OF GARNISH as something put on top of food once the food has been plated to prettify it, impart an aesthetic, and add flavor. Less frequently addressed is what is referred to as "internal garnish." For instance if you see pistachios and dried cherries in a pork *pâté en terrine*, those red and green hits of flavor are indeed a garnish—they're just on the inside of the food, not on top of it. You might fill a meatloaf with sun-dried tomatoes; these would be considered interior garnish. It's more than professional jargon; it helps us to think about what the food is doing. I like the term and use it here with the egg-yolk ravioli on page 151. The yolk is of course on the inside, and it adds flavor and visual drama to the finished dish when you cut into it.

Egg Ravioli with Chèvre, Brown Butter, and Thyme

SERVES 8 AS A FIRST COURSE OR 4 AS A LIGHT ENTRÉE

This is truly an egg-centric dish, with egg pasta, a yolk inside, and the ravioli sealed with the egg. I love putting a yolk inside pasta, perhaps my favorite way of serving the yolk on its own. It's a surprise to see the yolk spill out, and it flavors and enriches the dish. This is not a weekday meal preparation, but both the ravioli and sauce can be prepared ahead, refrigerated, and finished at the last minute. You can put anything you wish inside, or nothing. Cleveland chef Michael Symon used to serve an egg-yolk ravioli with ricotta, and he was the one who taught me the trick of putting a dot of cheese on top, which helps keep the yolk from breaking. Here I'm using a flavorful tangy cheese, but you could just as easily use caramelized onion, wilted spinach, or diced sautéed mushrooms—anything soft. One ravioli makes a great starting course; serve two for a more complete dish.

Fresh sheets of pasta for making ravioli are available in some markets, but you'll want to make your own because homemade is best. Some people find that the thinnest machine setting results in pasta too difficult to handle, so feel free to take the pasta only to the second-to-last setting. You can use a glass or ring cutter to turn these into attractive circular ravioli, but I make squares because I don't like to waste any pasta.

An important reminder: All yolks are not the same. Supermarket egg yolks are often incredibly delicate and quick to break. If you have these eggs, be gentle and make nice soft nests of cheese and onion.

2 teaspoons vegetable oil

1 Spanish onion, thinly sliced

2 ounces/60 grams chèvre, at room temperature

1 tablespoon milk or cream, at room temperature

Salt and freshly ground black pepper

½ recipe All-Purpose Pasta (page 97), rolled to the thinnest pasta machine setting and cut into four sheets (18 by 4½ inches/46 by 11 centimeters)

8 egg yolks (reserve some egg white for brushing the pasta; freeze the rest for another use)

¼ cup/60 grams butter

½ cup/60 grams slivered almonds

2 garlic cloves, minced

1 tablespoon fresh thyme, plus a few branches

Heat the oil in a small saucepan over medium-low heat and add the onion. Cook, stirring occasionally, until the onion is deeply caramelized, even mushy. This can take a couple of hours depending on how you wish to monitor heat. (You can make a big batch for soup and other uses and freeze them in individual containers ahead of time, if you wish.)

Combine the chèvre with the milk and salt and pepper to taste, and mash the cheese with a fork to combine the ingredients and make the cheese more spreadable.

Lay two sheets of pasta on a well-floured surface. Make a mark every 4½ inches/11 centimeters along the length of the pasta to designate each ravioli (for a total of 4 bottoms on one sheet and 4 tops on the other). Spread a teaspoon or two of the chèvre mixture in the center of each ravioli on one sheet only. Spread a teaspoon or two of caramelized onion on top of the chèvre, making a deep divot in the center where the yolk will rest (the yolk will slip off if you don't make the nest deep enough). Place a yolk on each bed of cheese and onion. Put another dab of the chèvre on top of the yolk.

Brush a little egg white on the pasta around the garnish so that the top will adhere. Lay the remaining sheet of pasta over the yolks, pressing down in the center and working outward to seal in the yolk while pressing out air bubbles. Using a pastry wheel (fluted if you have one) or a knife, cut the ravioli as you wish. If necessary, use a needle to poke holes in the ravioli and press the air out (otherwise the air, expanding from the heat of the boiling water, will make the ravioli float; if this happens, flip them carefully or press them below the surface so that the pasta cooks evenly). Repeat with the remaining two sheets of pasta and filling ingredients.

Bring a pot of water to a boil over high heat, adding enough salt so that it tastes like seasoned soup (2 to 3 tablespoons per gallon). Boil the ravioli till tender, 2½ to 3 minutes. Remove with a slotted spoon and transfer to a colander to drain. (The pasta can be made to this point a day in advance. Chill the ravioli completely in an ice bath, then transfer to a paper towel–lined plate. Cover with plastic wrap and store in the refrigerator. Bring the ravioli to room temperature before proceeding.)

Combine the butter and almonds in a large sauté pan, preferably nonstick, over medium-high heat. When the butter is melted, add the garlic and thyme branches. Cook until the butter begins to froth. Add the cooked ravioli, in batches if necessary, and carefully flip the pasta or spoon the melted butter over the top. When the ravioli are heated through, remove them to serving plates, spoon some browned butter and almonds over the top, and garnish with thyme leaves. Serve immediately.

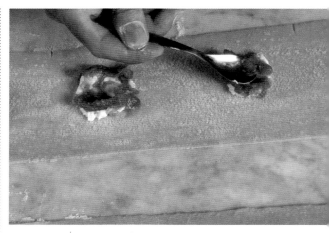

1. / *Make a bed of cheese and caramelized onion on the pasta, leaving a divot in it for the egg to nestle in.*

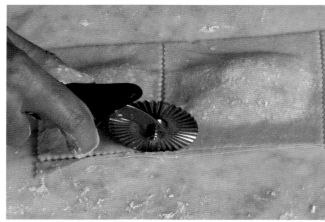

4. / *I like fluted edges and so trim the ravioli with a fluted pastry wheel, but a knife will also do the trick.*

7. / *Lift the ravioli out of the water with a large strainer or spider.*

/ Place a yolk on the cheese and onion, and add another dab of cheese on to prevent the yolk from breaking when you lay the top sheet of pasta on it.

3. / Lay the top sheet of pasta over the yolks.

5. / The filled and shaped ravioli, ready to cook.

6. / Boil the ravioli.

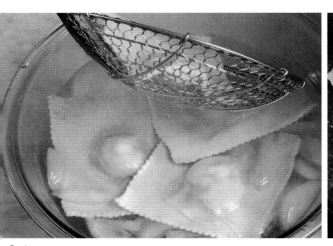

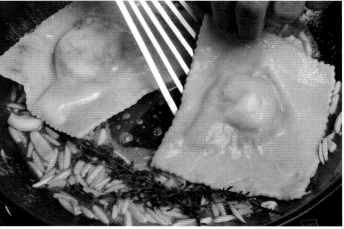

8. / Chill them in a water bath if you aren't going to serve them right away. Otherwise they can go straight into the finishing pan.

9. / The ravioli are finished in brown butter, with garlic, almonds, and thyme.

Egg / Separated / Yolk / Raw

Enricher

IN THE FOLLOWING RECIPES THE YOLK IS considered an ingredient because it enhances the other ingredients that accompany it. Rather than transforming the other ingredients, here it blends with them to add depth and richness. First, used raw, it enriches a Caesar dressing—though as I note, the egg yolk can be seen as both ingredient and tool in this form of vinaigrette. It can also be cooked and used to enrich a sauce, as in carbonara or in *blanquette de veau*, where it's combined with cream to create what's called a liaison. It's important not to cook the dish too hard after the liaison is added or the yolk will solidify and make your dish look curdled.

Caesar Dressing for Crisp Romaine Lettuce and Croutons

SERVES 4

I had my first real Caesar salad at the old Escoffier Room at the Culinary Institute of America, a restaurant dedicated to the classics. A Caesar salad for two was prepared tableside by a culinary student, who mixed the dressing in the wooden bowl before adding the lettuce. She mashed the garlic and anchovy with lemon juice to a paste, added the egg yolk and oil. She did an expert job of it, demonstrating how simple a vinaigrette can and should be. She also showed me the best way to dress a salad, by adding the lettuce to the dressing rather than pouring the dressing onto the lettuce (alternatively, you can pour the vinaigrette around the sides of the bowl while tossing the lettuce to avoid overdressing it; in either case, you want to allow the lettuce to pick up the dressing rather than get drowned in it). My cousin Rob makes a similar show of the Caesar, grandly dropping the yolk into the bowl. So it is both a show-offy salad and an easy salad for daily consumption. And it is the yolk that is the main feature of this dressing, enriching the dressing and, depending on how you mix it, making it very creamy by emulsifying the oil into the lemon juice. The flavors of garlic and anchovy should be subtle, present but not overpowering.

This is a staple dressing in our house. I use a hand blender with a chopper attachment for the mixing, allowing the salt to dissolve and the garlic to macerate in the lemon juice to soften its flavor. I don't measure; I just mix, taste, and add more oil till it's right. If I want it very creamy, I add a drop of oil first and thoroughly blend it, which establishes the emulsification, then add the remaining oil as necessary. The anchovies can be replaced in a pinch with ½ teaspoon good fish sauce.

Juice of ½ lemon (about 2 tablespoons)

1 large garlic clove, minced to a paste

Aggressive pinch of salt

Freshly ground black pepper

2 anchovies, minced to a paste

1 egg yolk

½ cup/120 milliliters vegetable oil, plus more if needed

1 pound/450 grams romaine lettuce, cut or torn into bite-size pieces

1 to 1½ cups/30 to 45 grams croutons

For a traditional hand-blended Caesar dressing, combine the lemon juice, garlic, and salt in a large salad bowl and let sit for 5 to 45 minutes. Whisk in the pepper, anchovies, egg yolk, and oil until they are thoroughly incorporated. Taste and add more oil if necessary.

For a very creamy Caesar, combine the lemon juice, garlic, and salt in the chopper attachment of a hand blender and let sit for 5 to 45 minutes. Add plenty of freshly ground pepper, the anchovies, and the yolk and pulse once or twice to combine. Add a single drop of oil and pulse and blend thoroughly to disperse it. Add half of the remaining oil and blend till it's well incorporated. Add the remaining oil and blend till it's thick. Taste and add more oil if necessary.

Add the lettuce to the dressing in the bowl (or pour the dressing made with a hand blender along the sides of the bowl as described in the headnote). Toss to distribute the dressing, garnish with the croutons, and serve.

Blanquette de Veau

SERVES 4

Veal stew in a white sauce, that's all blanquette de veau *is. And it's fantastic. My love of it again harks back to my days in the kitchens of the Culinary Institute of America. The class I was covering was about to prepare food for a grand buffet, the pre-graduation dinner where the revered president, Ferdinand Metz, made it a point to dine. Chef-instructor Rudy Smith, an excellent teacher and gifted cook, said that when Mr. Metz ate stew, it was always this highly refined stew. "Nobody eats before Mr. Metz," Chef Smith told us. "Make sure you know the whole menu. Be proud of what you know; share it with him. One thing you should not do is try to bullshit the man."*

So from that point on, blanquette de veau *became a dish of great distinction for me, a humble but refined stew preferred by this eminent chef, who had once plied his trade at Le Pavillon, the restaurant that made French cuisine the benchmark of fine dining in America. The delicate veal is first blanched to prevent coagulated protein from compromising the white beef stock–based sauce, which is enriched with a mixture of cream and our featured ingredient, the yolk—together known as a liaison. The liaison has the same effect as finishing a sauce with butter* (monté au beurre), *but it is looser and lighter.*

I once thought that the yolk thickened the sauce as it heated, but it doesn't—something I learned when I demonstrated this dish in public, watching the egg cook and curdle in my lovely sauce. It only enriches, so the sauce should be as thick as you wish it to be before you finish it with the liaison; the liaison enacts a textural change but not a thickening one. It's a satin gown.

I don't recommend making blanquette de veau *with store-bought broth—the quality of the stock is just too important to this dish. I prefer white beef or veal stock—that is, stock from blanched rather than roasted bones—though of course it works with stock made from roasted bones.*

1½ pounds/675 grams veal stew meat

1 Spanish onion, cut into medium dice

4 tablespoons/60 grams butter

Salt

½ cup/120 milliliters dry white wine

1 quart/1 liter rich white beef stock

1 pound/450 grams button mushrooms, quartered

16 to 20 pearl onions, blanched and peeled (about 1 cup)

¼ cup/35 grams flour

About 1 teaspoon fresh lemon juice or white wine vinegar

½ cup/120 milliliters heavy cream

3 egg yolks

Hot buttered egg noodles, for serving

1 tablespoon minced fresh parsley, for garnish

Put the veal in a pot and cover with water. Bring the water to a boil over high heat, then strain immediately and rinse the veal under cold water till clean and chilled.

In a medium saucepan over medium heat, sauté the Spanish onion in ½ tablespoon of the butter, giving it a four-finger pinch of salt, till it's completely tender but not browned, a few minutes. Add the wine and bring it to a simmer.

Add the blanched veal and stock, add a couple four-finger pinches of salt, and simmer until the meat is tender, 60 to 90 minutes. (This can be done 3 days before serving and refrigerated till you want to finish it.) The stock should reduce by about a quarter during this time. Cover and keep warm till you're ready to finish the dish.

While the veal is cooking, sauté the mushrooms over medium heat in ½ tablespoon of the butter till tender. Add the mushrooms and pearl onions to the stew 20 minutes before it finishes.

Meanwhile, melt the remaining 3 tablespoons butter in a small sauté pan over medium heat. When some of the water has cooked off, bubbling out of the butter, add the flour and cook, stirring gently, till it forms a loose paste (a roux) and some of the raw flour smell is gone. You want to cook it, without coloring it, till it smells like piecrust. Allow the roux to cool.

Return the meat to a simmer if it's not already there. Whisk in the roux and simmer, skimming any foam that collects on the surface, for 5 minutes. Taste for seasoning. Add more salt if it needs it and a few drops of lemon juice or white wine vinegar.

Whisk together the cream and the yolks and stir the mixture gently into the thickened liquid. Allow the stew to come back up to heat, just below a simmer, and serve immediately over egg noodles, garnishing with the parsley.

Chicken Fricassee

SERVES 4

A fricassee is similar to a blanquette in that the meat is sautéed first, then finished in the sauce. The difference is that no pains are taken for absolute refinement in a fricassee. Chicken and onion are cooked together, stock or water is added and thickened, and the dish is finished with the liaison. I like this dish precisely because it's a simple, rustic stew made voluptuous by the refined cream-yolk liaison. The all-purpose sauce can be varied any number of ways by adding spices—curry, paprika—to the chicken before adding the stock.

1 Spanish onion, cut into medium dice

2 carrots, peeled and cut into medium dice (optional if using stock)

4 tablespoons/60 grams butter

Salt

8 boneless skinless chicken thighs, cut into bite-size pieces

1 cup/240 milliliters dry white wine

1 quart/1 liter homemade chicken stock or water

2 bay leaves (optional if using stock)

1 pound/450 grams button mushrooms, quartered

16 to 20 pearl onions, blanched and peeled (about 1 cup)

¼ cup/35 grams flour

½ cup/120 milliliters heavy cream

3 egg yolks

Hot buttered egg noodles, for serving

1 tablespoon minced fresh parsley, for garnish

In a medium saucepan over medium heat, sauté the onion and carrot (if using) in ½ tablespoon of the butter, giving them a four-finger pinch of salt, until tender but not browned. Add the chicken and cook until the meat has lost all its pinkness, 3 to 5 minutes. Add the wine and bring to a simmer, then add the stock, bay leaves (if using), and another four-finger pinch of salt. Simmer until the chicken is tender, 30 minutes or so.

While the chicken is cooking, sauté the mushrooms over medium heat in ½ tablespoon of the butter till tender. Add the mushrooms and pearl onions to the stew.

Meanwhile, melt the remaining 3 tablespoons butter in a small sauté pan over medium heat. When some of the water has cooked off, bubbling out of the butter, add the flour and cook, stirring gently, till it forms a loose paste (a roux), and some of the raw flour smell is gone. You want to cook it, without coloring it, till it smells like piecrust. Allow the roux to cool.

Return the meat to a simmer if it's not already there. Whisk in the roux and simmer, skimming any foam that collects on the surface, for 5 minutes. Taste for seasoning and add more salt if it needs it.

Whisk together the cream and the yolks and stir the mixture gently into the thickened liquid. Allow the stew to come back up to heat, just below a simmer, and serve immediately over egg noodles, garnishing with the parsley.

Tool

Mayonnaise

ONE OF THE EGG YOLK'S STAR TURNS IS ITS capacity to emulsify fat into water—that is, separate the infinitesimal orbs of oil (created by a mechanical beating or blending of that oil) between thin sheets of water. This is how a fluid, translucent vegetable oil becomes an opaque, semisolid sauce. When flavor is added to it, it becomes a sauce of wonder—simply lemon juice and salt is enough to make it worthy of the gods. Spike it with cayenne, or use lime juice in place of the lemon, and you're riffing like a jazz artist. Get the yolk hot and fluffy before adding the fat and you're moving into the territory of the great French emulsified butter sauces.

But we're getting ahead of ourselves.

First, the mayonnaise basics. Foremost is to recognize that the jar of Hellmann's you get off the grocery store shelf is indeed mayonnaise, but it is different enough from homemade mayonnaise that I feel it's incumbent upon cooks to refer to the mayonnaise we buy by its brand name, and to homemade mayonnaise as "homemade mayon-naise" or "my own mayonnaise." Or maybe we could just shorten it to "my-own-aise." They are different products. I personally like Hellmann's for some uses, such as a fried-egg sandwich (page 31). But nothing like the mayonnaise you make at home is available at any store.

Second, there are several ways to make mayonnaise: whisk and bowl, mortar and pestle, hand blender with blade attachment, hand blender with whisk attachment.

Finally, the key to mayonnaise is twofold: you must have yolk, but the amount isn't critical, and you must have water or something water-based (e.g.,

lemon juice), and that amount *is* critical; it's what holds the sauce together. Too much oil relative to the water and the sauce can break, turning back into the consistency of oil.

What the yolk adds is lecithin. As I wrote earlier, this is one badass little molecule. It's got a fat-friendly side and a water-friendly side. The fat-friendly side embeds in the oil droplets and the water-friendly side connects with the water, strengthening the barrier that maintains the emulsion. Harold McGee notes in *On Food and Cooking* that a single yolk has enough lecithin to emulsify many, many cups of oil (provided there is enough water). The amount of water needed is also somewhat variable, depending on the power of your emulsifying tool. I've found that you need about one part water for every twenty parts oil, or 1 ounce water for every 2½ cups oil, or 10 grams water for 200 grams oil (see how easy recipes become when you use metric measurements?). If you see your mayonnaise looking like it's going to break on you, drizzle in a little water (knowing whether you need a little more water is a matter of intuition, experience, and fear). You can't break your mayonnaise by adding too much water, but you can make it too thin—in which case you'll have to emulsify more oil into it and adjust the seasonings till it returns to the consistency and flavor you want.

The only other point that should be noted is that salt doesn't dissolve readily in fat. I always add salt to the water-based element so that it dissolves there and spreads evenly through the sauce.

Other than that, one of the world's greatest sauces is, start to finish, minutes away.

The most controlled way to make mayonnaise successfully is with a whisk, but I almost never do that because it takes more time. The fastest way to make mayonnaise is with a hand blender in a 2-cup/480-milliliter glass measuring cup. Provided the blade reaches near enough to the bottom of the measuring cup, a mayonnaise can be created 30 seconds after assembling your ingredients. The only drawback is that you're limited to making about ¾ cup/180 milliliters of mayonnaise before it breaks. To make it this way, put the water, salt, and yolk in the measuring glass and, with the blade running, allow a drop or two of oil into the cup, then slowly pour in the rest of the oil, pumping the running blade up and down until you've added all your oil. You should have a thick mayonnaise that stands in peaks.

Using the whisk attachment on a hand blender in a 1-quart/1-liter glass measuring cup is just as easy, and you can make plenty at a time.

Basic Mayonnaise

MAKES 1 CUP/240 MILLILITERS

This is a simple, delicious, all-purpose mayonnaise that makes everything better, from egg salad to spreads on sandwiches (a basic BLT is out of this world when made with your own mayonnaise). Spoon it over asparagus or boiled cauliflower, eat it with artichokes, mix it into chopped hard-cooked egg, make a lobster roll with it. Always taste and adjust the seasoning to your liking, paying special attention to the acidity level and how you may be using it.

1 tablespoon fresh lemon juice

1 teaspoon water

Salt

1 egg yolk

1 cup/240 milliliters vegetable oil

Put the lemon juice, water, and a four-finger pinch of salt in a 2-cup/480-milliliter glass measuring cup. Whisk them together to dissolve the salt. Add the yolk and whisk to combine. While whisking, vigorously add one, two, then three drops of oil, then add the remaining oil in a steady stream, whisking continuously. You can stop midway through if your arm gets tired; the emulsion won't fall apart.

Alternatively, you can use a hand blender. Let a drop or two of the oil fall off the tip of a spoon into the moving yolk-lemon mixture to establish the emulsion. Once it's fairly stable, add the rest of the oil in a thin, steady stream. If it starts to get too thick, add a sprinkle of water.

Use right away, or store in a covered container in the refrigerator for up to 3 days.

VARIATION: To make aioli, add one or two smashed garlic cloves and use olive oil or a mixture of vegetable and olive oils. Use it the same day you make it.

Lemon-Shallot Mayonnaise

MAKES ABOUT ¾ CUP/180 MILLILITERS

This is my go-to mayonnaise for just about anything that mayonnaise goes well with. It's so good you almost want to eat it with a spoon—and my mom sometimes does! I love it with artichokes (page 16) and egg salad (page 9), but it goes with pretty much anything—fish, chicken, or any number of vegetables. It should be made the day you want to eat it; it can sit for a day in the fridge, but the shallots give it an off flavor after too many unappreciated hours.

1 tablespoon plus 2 teaspoons fresh lemon juice

1 tablespoon minced shallot

½ teaspoon salt

1 teaspoon water

1 egg yolk

Pinch of cayenne pepper

¾ cup/180 milliliters vegetable oil

Combine the shallot with 1 tablespoon of the lemon juice and set aside while you make the mayonnaise.

Combine the remaining 2 teaspoons lemon juice, the salt, water, yolk, and cayenne in a bowl (or in a large glass measuring cup if using a hand blender, page 161, which is my preferred method). Whisk them together to dissolve the salt. Whisking continuously, add one, two, then three drops of oil to establish the emulsion, then add the remaining oil in a thin, steady stream, until all of the oil has been incorporated and the mayonnaise is thick and sumptuous. Stir in the shallot and lemon juice. If using the hand-blender method, you can add the shallot after mixing for a chunkier mayo, or blend the shallot with the yolk for a smooth mayo.

FIXING A BROKEN MAYONNAISE

If you make mayonnaise, every now and then it's going to break on you. It may happen quickly, go from thick to soupy in a blink, or it may just look a little thin and grainy. But that's no reason to throw it away. Put 2 teaspoons water into a clean bowl or vessel, and pour the broken mayonnaise—a drop or two at first, then in a thin stream—into the water, whisking continuously. If you want to add more yolk to the 2 teaspoons water before re-emulsifying, for safety, that's fine, but it's not usually necessary.

Grilled Chicken Salad with Chipotle-Lime Mayonnaise

SERVES 4

In the same way that deviled eggs are better when you use your own mayonnaise, so is an ordinary chicken salad elevated to exquisite heights when you bend your mayo to your will, as with a dynamic chipotle-lime version, scented with cumin. Of course the mayo features minced shallot, which is a small kitchen miracle in its versatility; when macerated in citrus it is a beguiling aromatic in all emulsified sauces.

We grill a lot of chicken in the summer, and we often have leftovers, to which this is put to use. The flavors of the grill mix well with the smoky heat of the chipotle and lime. Of course any cooked chicken will work—even, sigh, baked boneless chicken breast. (Indeed, this may be one of a handful of ways of redeeming this sorry staple of American culinary culture.) But the meat of preference here would be skin-on thighs, grilled. Remember that while a layer of fat undergirds the skin, the skin itself is mainly protein, and very flavorful, and can be finely minced and added to the salad.

This makes a terrific lunch and is an excellent dinner when the weather is so hot you don't want to use the stove. It's also a great example of how leftovers become standout main courses with the help of mayonnaise you make and flavor yourself. The chipotle-lime mayo would also work well with roasted or grilled beef, pork, or lamb. A vegetarian version could be made by swapping in baked potatoes for the meat.

The one element that would be missing from this rich, salty, acidic, spicy flavor combination is sweetness, so I'm adding sautéed onion for this final element of balance. If you're making this on the fly, you can omit the onion, but it's really amazing how much depth of flavor a cooked onion brings to just about any dish. I season the mayo with a little fish sauce, another umami ingredient that provides additional depth (but which you shouldn't be able to actually taste).

Serve the chicken salad on kaiser rolls or on butter lettuce with a toasted baguette on the side.

1 tablespoon fresh lime juice

1 teaspoon water

½ teaspoon salt

¼ teaspoon fish sauce (optional)

2 chipotle peppers in adobo sauce, seeded and finely minced

1 egg yolk

¾ cup/180 milliliters vegetable oil

1 pound/450 grams grilled chicken thighs, boneless, roughly chopped, and at room temperature

½ Spanish onion, cut into medium dice and cooked in a little oil over medium-high heat till tender and a little browned at the edges, then cooled (optional but recommended)

2 to 3 celery ribs, cut into small dice

Butter lettuce

4 kaiser rolls or 1 baguette, toasted if you wish

To make the mayonnaise, combine the lime juice, water, salt, fish sauce (if using), chipotles, and yolk in a bowl (or in a large glass measuring cup if using a hand blender, page 161, which is my preferred method). Whisk them together to dissolve the salt. Whisking continuously, add one, two, then three drops of oil to establish the emulsion, then add the remaining oil in a steady stream, until all of the oil has been incorporated and the mayonnaise is thick and sumptuous. Taste. It should be almost like a vinaigrette and plenty spicy, so add more lime juice or extra chipotles if you wish.

Combine the chicken, onion (if using), celery, and mayonnaise and stir to mix. Taste and season with more salt, chipotles, or lime juice until it's perfect. Serve with the lettuce and rolls or bread.

Sauce

Pasta Carbonara

SERVES 4

When people tell me they don't have time to cook dinner for the family, I suggest this staple of the Italian kitchen and all-around favorite for its simplicity and deeply satisfying impact. This is one of my go-to meals when I want something fast, delicious, and satisfying. All of the elements—salty smoky bacon, bacon fat, pasta, cheese—are bound together by the yolk. Reputed to be served to coal-dusty miners returning from work for their meal (hence the name), this dish is a paragon of Italian simplicity and economy. The cured pork in Italy would be pancetta or guanciale, *salted, dry-cured hog jowl; both work well and each alters the finished dish slightly. Pancetta lacks smokiness;* guanciale *has a rich flavor, but less meat and more fat. Bacon is what is common here in the States. All are delicious. I prefer pork belly for its perfect meat-to-fat ratio.*

Pasta carbonara luxuriates in the amazing egg yolk, which is the primary sauce ingredient. Traditionally, there's no other liquid, just yolk, but I like to add a little half-and-half; this goes outside tradition and makes purists bristle, but the half-and-half facilitates the spreading of the yolk throughout the pasta and keeps the pasta juicy rather than sticky. It should be a little liquidy when it receives the grated cheese, with the heat from the fat and pasta lightly cooking the yolk.

As a rule of thumb, I use 2 yolks per serving and an equal quantity of half-and-half by weight (I often make this just for Donna and myself—it's a great quick lunch). And remember that the bacon can be rendered as many as 3 days before finishing the dish, cooled, and stored, covered, in the refrigerator, so that you could literally finish the entire dish in the time it takes to boil water and cook the pasta. I like to use thin spaghetti, but any shape will work. I usually just cook a whole box and save one-quarter of it for another use. An interesting variation on this dish, which we did for Eric Ripert's book A Return to Cooking, *was to make a risotto in the bacon pan and simply finish with a garnish of one whole yolk in the center.*

8 ounces/225 grams bacon (or pancetta or *guanciale*), cut into strips

12 ounces/340 grams dried thin spaghetti

8 egg yolks

½ to 1 cup/170 to 225 milliliters half-and-half

Salt to taste (about ½ teaspoon, but less to none if the bacon is very salty)

2 to 2¼ cups/170 to 225 grams grated Parmigiano-Reggiano

Freshly ground black pepper

1 to 2 tablespoons minced fresh parsley (optional)

In a large sauté pan, render the bacon till it's crisp on the outside and tender inside (the process is easiest if you start the bacon in water over high heat, then turn the heat to medium-low when the water cooks off).

Meanwhile, bring a large pot of salted water to a boil and cook the pasta till it's done to your liking; drain.

Remove the sizzling bacon from the heat. Add the pasta and toss it in the bacon fat till it's nicely coated. Whisk the yolks and half-and-half to combine; pour the mixture over the pasta, continuing to toss it. Taste it and add salt if needed. When the pasta is uniformly coated with the sauce, add two-thirds of the cheese and toss again.

Serve, garnishing with the remaining cheese, plenty of freshly ground pepper, and parsley, if desired.

Tool

Hollandaise and Béarnaise

IN THE SAME WAY THAT AN EGG YOLK (combined with some water) can transform ordinary vegetable oil into a creamy, ethereal sauce, so too can it work its magic on butter. I'm talking about the emulsified butter sauces so popular in the French repertoire that most carry French names (such as their word for Holland, or the name of the mountainous region of Gascony in southwestern France, Béarn, home of the legendary d'Artagnan).

I grew up watching my mom make béarnaise sauce straight out of Julia Child's seminal *Mastering the Art of French Cooking*. She raised it to the level of a one-on-one sport, my mom against the sauce. When she got into the ring with tarragon and yolks and butter, we all drew near, watching her whip that sauce. At the time we knew only that the more butter you got in there the better the sauce, but too much and it could break on you for whatever reasons decreed by the cooking gods. So when the sauce was perfect, and she risked yet another chunk of butter, you could hear gasps from the crowd.

Which is why I love béarnaise sauce.

When my parents' parties went on so long that I woke and descended the stairs to Doris Grayson's laughter, signaling to the guests that it was time to leave (as if the daylight weren't enough), Mom would sensibly repair to bed, but Dad would make the two of us eggs Benedict, poached eggs with hollandaise sauce, the famed dish created by the chef of the Waldorf Hotel as a restorative for a hungover Mr. Benedict. After breakfast, instead of sleeping after the long night of bibulous partying, Dad would be out there mowing the lawn, thereby teaching me at an early age the restorative powers conveyed by a proper eggs Benedict.

Which is why I love hollandaise sauce.

The emulsified butter sauce strikes fear into the hearts of home cooks. It should not—it's nothing more than a hot mayonnaise with more yolk for richness. It can be made exactly like a mayonnaise, with a hand blender, a whisk, or a countertop blender. And, really, any kind of fat can be used. To do it the classical French way, use clarified butter. In my last book, I used schmaltz (rendered chicken fat with onion) to make a variation on béarnaise. If someone is allergic to dairy products, pity the poor soul, but you can make a hollandaise with warm vegetable oil instead of butter.

The single element that distinguishes a hot emulsified sauce from a cold emulsified sauce is that the heat is actively expelling water from the sauce; as water is the critical element holding everything together, losing too much of it can allow all the fat droplets to group together, breaking your sauce. Of course the heat can also cook the egg, turning it to curds in your sauce, which is why many recipes recommend cooking the sauce over simmering water as opposed to the direct dry heat of flame against metal.

So, now that you know all of the forces working for and against you before you step into the ring with an emulsified butter sauce, you can relax. Have a glass of wine. About 20 minutes or up to an hour before you are ready to serve, make your sauce, as guests gather around, not like sports fans at a boxing match, but rather as an audience amazed by your cool ease with the notoriously "difficult" French butter sauce.

There are three components to these sauces:

the flavoring, the egg-water mixture, and the fat. How you use each determines the nature of the sauce. The classical method is to make a vinegar and aromatic reduction first, simmering herbs, shallot, and peppercorns and straining this into your pot with the yolks. But you can simply cook shallots and freshly ground pepper and vinegar and add this without straining. Next, cook the yolks and flavoring liquid, whipping them over gentle heat until they're warm and fluffy (when in doubt, it's better to undercook; if they go past 180°F/85°C, they're going to scramble). When they're done, slowly add your butter, whipping continuously. Mom used to throw in cold chunks of whole butter; these both cooled the sauce and added more water to it. I like to melt the butter and add it warm to the warm eggs.

I'll give an example of two methods here (though the hand-blender method used for mayonnaise can also be used): a blender hollandaise, first written about, to my knowledge, by Julia in her aforementioned book, and then a classical béarnaise sauce with a true reduction.

REUSING LEFTOVER BÉARNAISE, HOLLANDAISE, OR ANY EMULSIFIED BUTTER SAUCE

If you have leftover sauce, don't blame the sauce; I'm sure it was excellent. But don't throw it out! Put it in a glass measuring cup, cover with plastic, and refrigerate for up to 7 days. When you want to reuse, melt it in a microwave, and whisk into it 1 teaspoon water for every ⅓ cup/75 milliliters leftover sauce you are re-emulsifying. It should return to its luxurious delicacy in moments. If you need to heat it further, do so gently over low heat, and be careful not to cook it. Serve it over scrambled eggs, toast, or a steak sandwich.

Blender Hollandaise Sauce

MAKES ABOUT ¾ CUP/180 MILLILITERS

*This quick and nearly foolproof method is just
what the doctor orders on a Sunday morning when
efficiency is to be desired in getting your Eggs Benedict
(page 47) on the table. However, if you want to
prepare hollandaise in the traditional fashion, follow
the recipe for béarnaise sauce on page 170, omitting
the dried tarragon from the reduction and adding a
teaspoon or two of lemon juice to the finished sauce
instead of fresh tarragon.*

2 tablespoons fresh lemon juice

¼ teaspoon salt (½ teaspoon if using
unsalted butter)

3 egg yolks

½ cup/110 grams butter, melted

Put the lemon juice, salt, and yolks in a blender.
Turn the blender to medium-high, then pour the
hot butter in a steady stream into the running
blender until all the butter is added and the sauce
is thick.

. / By far the easiest and fastest way to separate an egg is by hand. (Please don't get me started on those egg separators for sale; the best one ever invented is at the end of your arm.) This method works especially well when you're doing a lot of eggs, as here, with a recipe that calls for eight. Gently scoop up one egg.

Separate your fingers enough for the white to slip through but not the yolk. It's to leave on the white coils, or chalazae. If you want to pinch them off, be aware that the yolk usually breaks when you do, so hold your hand over a bowl.

3. / Pass the yolk back and forth between your hands until all the white has fallen away, then drop the yolk into another bowl. Separating the eight eggs should take less than a minute.

Traditional Béarnaise Sauce

MAKES ABOUT 1 CUP/240 MILLILITERS

This is my favorite sauce in the world. It wouldn't be out of place on baked white fish, but I like to serve this elegant French sauce on a great American hamburger. I recommend going to the trouble of grinding your own beef chuck, which has a goodly amount of fat in it. Rinse it and pat it dry, then give it a good salting an hour before grinding (as for Steak Tartare, page 212). Garnish the burger with butter lettuce and caramelized onion, or serve as is. It's OK to use store-ground chuck, too—the focus here is on the sauce and how well it complements the grilled beef. (Needless to say, you can use this sauce on any cut of grilled beef.)

I'm going to give the premier method and ingredients here for the finest béarnaise (minus the clarified butter, which is traditional but unnecessary), but you could also just adapt the blender hollandaise recipe on page 168 by adding 1 tablespoon dried tarragon to the butter before melting it (which is what I do when there is no fresh tarragon to be had).

FOR THE REDUCTION:

10 black peppercorns, cracked with the flat side of a knife

¼ cup/60 milliliters white wine vinegar or tarragon vinegar

1½ tablespoons dried tarragon

1 tablespoon minced shallot

¼ cup/60 milliliters water

FOR THE BÉARNAISE:

2 egg yolks

2 teaspoons water

1 teaspoon fresh lemon juice

1 teaspoon salt

1 cup/225 grams butter, melted

⅓ cup/10 grams minced fresh tarragon

To make the reduction, heat the peppercorns in a small sauté pan over medium heat until you can smell them. Add the vinegar, tarragon, and shallot to the pan and simmer until almost all of the liquid is gone. Add the water, return to a simmer, then remove the pan from the heat.

To make the sauce, combine the yolks, water, lemon juice, and salt in a saucepan (a 3-quart/ 2.8-liter saucier is best for whisking). Strain the reduction through a fine-mesh sieve into the saucepan, pressing on the ingredients to squeeze out more liquid. Whisk to combine, then hold over medium heat, whisking continuously and occasionally removing the pan from the heat to avoid cooking the eggs. You're looking for a fluffy, ribbony mixture, warm but not hot. Reduce the heat to low.

Using a spoon, let a few drops of melted butter fall into the yolks while whisking vigorously to establish the emulsion, then whisk in the remaining butter. The butter solids and water at the bottom can be added or not. (If the sauce is very thick, or if you've cooked a lot of liquid out of it, endangering its stability, the water will stabilize it.) If the sauce is too thin, continue cooking it, carefully, until it falls thickly from the whisk. (You can make the blender version by adding the hot reduction to the yolks in the blender and continuing to blend as you pour in the hot butter.)

Add the fresh tarragon and whisk to distribute it.

Serve on freshly grilled rare hamburgers (or other grilled beef or lean fish).

Custard Sauce

Crème Anglaise

MAKES ABOUT 3½ CUPS/840 MILLILITERS

This is the workhorse sauce of the dessert kitchen, the all-purpose vanilla sauce, which can be transformed into numerous other preparations. It scarcely differs from the crème brûlée on the next page except in the way it's cooked. Indeed, you can enrich a crème anglaise by replacing half the milk with cream, a strategy I've seen in many kitchens. Feel free to do this if you wish, though you may face the wrath of traditionalists. Vanilla sauce can be manipulated in various ways to different ends: cooked in a water bath, it's a custard; frozen, it's ice cream; thickened with flour or cornstarch, it becomes pastry cream; and as is, of course, it's a basic sauce to eat with cakes, soufflés, and other desserts. But at its heart it's simply egg yolks cooked with milk and sugar, flavored with vanilla.

3 cups/720 milliliters milk

Pinch of salt

1 vanilla bean, split lengthwise

¾ cup/150 grams sugar

9 egg yolks

Combine the milk, salt, and vanilla bean in a small saucepan and bring to a simmer over medium-high heat. Remove the pan from the heat and let the bean steep for 15 minutes. With a paring knife, scrape the seeds from the pod into the milk. (Put the empty pod in your sugar bowl or bag to gently infuse the sugar.)

Combine the sugar and yolks in a medium bowl and whisk vigorously for 30 seconds or so (this will help the sugar to begin dissolving and will also help the egg cook more evenly).

Fill a large bowl with half ice and half water, and float a second bowl in the ice bath. Set a fine-mesh strainer in the bowl.

Over medium heat, bring the milk back to a simmer, then pour it slowly into the yolks while whisking continuously. Pour the mixture back into the pan and continue stirring over medium heat until the mixture is slightly thick, or *nappé*—it should be pourable, but if you dip a spoon in it, it should be thick enough on the spoon to draw a line through. This will take 2 to 4 minutes.

Pour the sauce through the strainer into the bowl set in the ice bath. Stir the sauce with a rubber spatula until it is cold. Use right away or cover with plastic wrap, pressing down on the plastic so that it lies on the surface of the sauce, and refrigerate for up to 1 week.

Crème Brûlée

SERVES 4

This is as simple and perfect as a dessert gets. Because there are so few ingredients, their care is critical. Egg cooked fast and at high heat turns hard. Or it curdles, crosses its fleshy arms in anger at having been ill used. So you must treat the yolk with thoughtfulness, authority, and finesse. It's the yolk's richness and capacity to set as it heats the fluid dairy that make it the queen of this dessert and so many sauces.

I'm offering here a traditional crème brûlée, nothing but milk and cream, vanilla, and sugar brought together by the enveloping egg yolk. The yolk gathers these ingredients and works them in concert to create a sweet pudding with a crunchy burnt-sugar top. I always tap the top with my spoon to hear the click on the burnt, candied surface, and then tap a little harder to break through to the cream, a pleasure like a child's in stepping on the frozen surface of a puddle. I then scoop up the vanilla custard below, to combine on the palate smooth luxury and brittle melting sweetness.

A custard such as this requires gentle heat, thus a water bath, the self-regulating thermometer of H$_2$O, which will never go higher than 200°F/95°C in an oven set between 200° and 300°F/95° and 150°C. The water will remain below a boil if uncovered.

Please don't desecrate this lovely dessert with vanilla extract or fancy aromatics. Appreciate it for what it is: one of the perfect dishes in the western repertoire.

1 cup/240 milliliters milk

1 cup/240 milliliters heavy cream

Pinch of salt

1 vanilla bean, split lengthwise

½ cup/100 grams plus ¼ cup/50 grams sugar

8 egg yolks

Preheat the oven to 300°F/150°C. Place four 4- to 5-ounce/120- to 150-milliliter ramekins in a large sauté pan or roasting pan and fill the pan so that the water comes three-quarters of the way up the sides of the ramekins. Remove the ramekins and place the pan of water in the oven.

Combine the milk, cream, salt, and vanilla bean in a small saucepan and bring to a simmer over medium-high heat. Remove the pan from the heat and let the bean steep for 15 minutes. With a paring knife, scrape the seeds from the pod into the milk-cream mixture. (Put the empty pod in your sugar bowl or bag to gently infuse the sugar.)

Combine ½ cup/100 grams of the sugar and the yolks in a medium bowl and whisk vigorously for 30 seconds or so (this will help the sugar begin to dissolve and will also help the egg cook more evenly). Slowly pour the cream mixture into the yolks while whisking continuously.

Pour the custard into the ramekins. Cover each with a piece of parchment paper followed by foil and put them in the water bath. Cook the custards until just set, about 30 minutes. Uncover them and allow to cool. (If you intend to serve them the following day, cover them again and refrigerate; remove them from the refrigerator several hours before serving to allow them to come to room temperature.)

Top each custard with enough of the remaining ¼ cup/50 grams sugar to coat the entire surface and pour off the excess. With a propane torch, heat the sugar till it melts, bubbles, and caramelizes—when it's cool, the browned sugar should create a delicate crust. Serve immediately.

Pastry Cream

MAKES ABOUT 3½ CUPS/840 MILLILITERS

To make a great pastry cream with which to fill profiteroles (page 105) or undergird a berry tart or layer a cake, simply thicken our all-purpose vanilla sauce with a milk-and-cornstarch slurry. Follow the instructions for crème anglaise on page 171, up through pouring the milk-egg mixture back into the pan. Before bringing it back up to heat, add 3 tablespoons cornstarch mixed with 3 tablespoons milk. Cook the sauce till it thickens, then, rather than straining it, simply submerge the pot in an ice bath to cool it and whip in 1 to 2 ounces/30 to 60 grams room-temperature butter while it's still warm enough to melt the butter. Keep stirring till the sauce has cooled. Refrigerate the pastry cream with plastic wrap pressed down on its surface so that it doesn't develop a skin.

Vanilla Ice Cream

MAKES ABOUT 3½ CUPS/840 MILLILITERS

This is, more or less, a crème brûlée cooked on the stovetop and then frozen, or a frozen crème anglaise, or a rich pastry cream that's thickened by freezing rather than with starch. The basic vanilla creams are all very similar, demonstrating the range of what can be done with the combination of dairy, sugar, and yolks. The yolks give the ice cream its beautiful color, richness, and depth of flavor.

1½ cups/360 milliliters milk

1½ cups/360 milliliters heavy cream

Pinch of salt

1 vanilla bean, split lengthwise

¾ cup/150 grams sugar

9 egg yolks

Combine the milk, cream, salt, and vanilla bean in a small saucepan and bring to a simmer over medium-high heat. Remove the pan from the heat and let the bean steep for 15 minutes. With a paring knife, scrape the seeds from the pod into the milk-cream mixture. (Put the empty pod in your sugar bowl or bag to gently infuse the sugar.)

Combine the sugar and yolks in a medium bowl and whisk vigorously for 30 seconds or so (this will help the sugar begin to dissolve and will also help the egg to cook more evenly).

Fill a large bowl with half ice and half water and float a second bowl in the ice bath. Set a fine-mesh strainer in the bowl.

Over medium heat, bring the milk-cream mixture back to a simmer, then pour it slowly into the yolks while whisking continuously. Pour the mixture back into the pan and continue stirring over medium heat until the mixture is slightly thick, or *nappé* (it should be pourable, but if you dip a spoon in it, it should be thick enough on the spoon to draw a line through. This will take 2 to 4 minutes.

Pour the sauce through the strainer into the bowl set in the ice bath. Stir the sauce with a rubber spatula until it is cold. Cover and refrigerate till it's thoroughly chilled, preferably overnight. The colder it is before going into the ice cream machine, the better.

Freeze according to your machine's instructions.

Poire Williams Sabayon

SERVES 4

This yolk-based dessert sauce is typically made with a sweet wine such as a sauterne or, in Italy, where it's called zabaglione, *with an Italian sweet wine such as marsala. For this recipe I used a Michigan-made pear eau de vie; you can also use Grand Marnier or another favorite brandy or liqueur.*

The sauce is made by whipping yolks, sugar, and wine over a double boiler until the yolks are cooked and the sauce has become thick and ribbony. It can be served as is in small cups, or poured over fruit or cake. You could also whip the egg whites with sugar and make Île Flottante *(page 200).*

4 egg yolks

¼ cup/50 grams sugar

Pinch of salt

¼ cup/60 milliliters pear eau de vie
(or other suitable spirit)

2 tablespoons water

1 teaspoon fresh lemon juice (optional)

Grated lemon zest, for garnish

In the top of a double boiler or a large metal bowl set over simmering water, combine all of the ingredients except the lemon zest and whisk continuously until the mixture is warm, has quadrupled in volume, and becomes a satiny, ribbony sauce, about 10 minutes. Remove from the heat and serve warm, garnished with grated lemon zest.

Part Six

Egg / Separated

The White

The egg white is an astonishing culinary lever. A mixture of a dozen or so proteins, water, and a few trace elements, it is designed to protect the yolk from anything dangerous, whether virus, bacterium, or predator. But the feats those proteins can achieve in the kitchen are as diverse as they are extraordinary.

Egg whites act as a binder for the Seafood Roulade (page 179) or any mousseline; they set cream for the Orange-Ginger Panna Cotta (page 187); they clarify stock for Turkey Consommé (page 185); and they lend body—and nutrition!—to cocktails, such as the Clover Club Cocktail (page 188). They can also be used as a garnish, and are a powerful leavening device.

The yolk is a kind of diva in the kitchen. The white is more akin to an Olympic gymnast—its range and power are nothing short of astonishing.

• • •

Binder

―――――――――――――――――――

Seafood Roulade with Scallops and Crab

MAKES 8 (3-OUNCE) PORTIONS

The foundation of this dish, a mousseline, is a fundamental preparation with a broad reach and infinite variations. A mousseline is simply a white meat or fish pureed with cream and bound by egg white—about two parts meat to one part cream, all of it bound with about 10 percent egg. Whole eggs can be used for richness, but for a very light, delicate mousseline I prefer egg whites only, which bind the meat and fat into a delicate but sliceable whole. The mousseline can be turned into pike quenelles or a ravioli stuffing of chicken with roasted garlic. It's most commonly used with fish because the lightness of the fat (cream) and texture (from the egg white) enhances the flavor of the fish without overpowering it.

I'm offering here a shrimp mousseline because shrimp reliably binds with the cream and egg for a great texture. Salmon makes a terrific mousseline, too. Scallops, by contrast, carry inconsistent levels of water based on how they've been stored, so the texture of the cooked mousseline can vary. But I love the flavor of scallops and their impeccable whiteness as a garnish, so I've included them in the roulade, along with lump crabmeat, which provides an excellent flavor parallel. For an even more dramatic preparation, steep ½ teaspoon crumbled saffron in the cream, then chill it, for a color that will make the interior crab and scallops especially vivid.

The roulade can be sliced and served cold with Lemon-Shallot Mayonnaise (page 162), which is how I prefer it. Or it can be sliced and gently sautéed in butter to warm through, then served with a light butter-and-lemon sauce (heat some lemon juice and shallot with a tablespoon of water or white wine and swirl in pats of butter) or a shellfish sauce made from the shrimp shells (as in the photo on page 181). This mixture can also be stuffed into sheep casings (chop the scallops) and poached, then sautéed for outstanding seafood sausages.

1 tablespoon butter

1 leek, white part only, finely chopped

1 pound/450 grams peeled, deveined shrimp

2 egg whites

1 teaspoon salt

1 cup/240 milliliters heavy cream

**4 ounces/120 grams scallops,
cut into chunks if large or whole if small**

4 ounces/120 grams lump crabmeat

2 tablespoons minced fresh chives

Heat the butter in a small sauté pan over medium heat. Add the leek and sauté until tender but not brown. Transfer to a bowl, cover, and refrigerate until chilled.

Puree the shrimp with the egg whites and salt in a food processor. With the machine running, slowly add half of the cream through the feed tube. The mixture should be stiff enough to shape. Continue adding the rest of the cream with the machine running.

Transfer the shrimp mousseline to a mixing bowl and add the chilled leeks, scallops, crab, and chives, gently folding to distribute everything evenly.

Wet your counter slightly and lay out a sheet of plastic wrap (use Glad wrap if you're concerned about cooking in plastic), at least 2 feet/60 centimeters long. Spoon the seafood mixture along the center of the plastic wrap. Fold the plastic wrap over the mousseline and roll it into a tube about 2½ inches/6 centimeters in diameter. Twist each end of the plastic wrap to form a tight roulade as you roll it on the counter. If it gets out of shape on you, unroll it onto a new sheet of plastic and start again.

Bring a large pot of water to 180°F/82°C. Drop the roulade into the water and weigh it down with an appropriately sized plate to keep it submerged. Cook the roulade, maintaining a water temperature of between 170° and 185°F/77° and 85°C, until an instant-read thermometer reads between 140° and 150°F/60° and 65°C when inserted into the center of the roulade, 45 to 50 minutes.

While the roulade is cooking, fill a large bowl with half ice and half water. When the roulade is done, submerge it in the ice bath until thoroughly chilled, 15 minutes or so. Remove the plastic wrap and serve (see the headnote for suggestions).

Seafood Roulade

1. / *Mousseline mise en place (clockwise from top left): cream, herbs, interior garnish (crabmeat, scallops, and leeks), salt, shrimp, and egg white.*

2. / *First, puree shrimp and egg white.*

5. / *Last, add the leeks and stir until the garnishes are uniformly distributed.*

6. / *Spread the mousseline onto plastic wrap to shape it.*

9. / *Roll the roulade, holding both ends of the plastic wrap, until it's a tight cylinder. It's now ready to poach.*

10. / *The roulade, cooked and removed from the plastic wrap.*

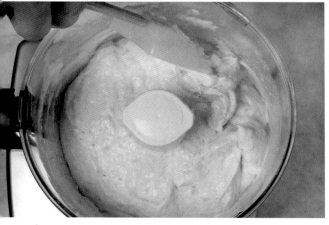

3. / *After you've slowly added the cream, with the blade running, the result will be a stiff shrimp paste, or mousseline.*

4. / *Remove the mousseline to a bowl and fold in the garnishes, here crabmeat and scallops.*

7. / *Form the roulade by shaping it into a cylinder.*

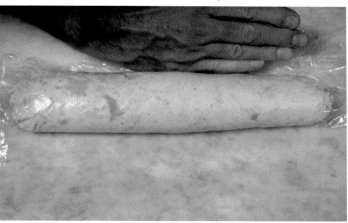

8. / *Press your hand or a flat edge such as a baking sheet into the cylinder to make it as tight as possible.*

11. / *Slice the roulade with a single forward stroke, if possible.*

12. / *These slices of roulade can be eaten cold, with some Lemon-Shallot Mayonnaise (page 162), or they can be sautéed if you'd like to serve them hot.*

1. / Whisk in the egg whites, then stir continuously with a flat-edged spoon to prevent sticking.

2. / Once the stock is hot, the egg whites will cook and rise to the surface.

3. / As the stock comes to a simmer, the egg wh will act as a filter.

4. / After the stock has cooked for 45 to 60 minutes, strain it through a coffee filter.

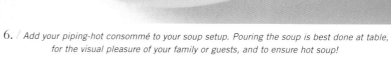

5. / Place your garnishes in a bowl. Both bowl and garnishes should be warm, if not hot.

6. / Add your piping-hot consommé to your soup setup. Pouring the soup is best done at table, for the visual pleasure of your family or guests, and to ensure hot soup!

Clarifier

Turkey Consommé

MAKES 8 (4-OUNCE) PORTIONS

One of the most amazing things that egg whites can do is clarify a cloudy stock into a crystal-clear elixir for what we call consommé. In culinary school we were taught to make a chicken consommé because, I suppose, chicken stock was so plentiful. We were taught that it should be crystal *clear. Here was how the school stated the standard of clarity: you should be able to read the date on a dime at the bottom of a gallon of it. I loved that. I wrote about it. Some people have emailed me photos of dimes in their soup.*

I've noted earlier that certain comments from chefs stick with you. I learned how to make chicken consommé in my first kitchen at the Culinary Institute of America from Michael Pardus. In my last kitchen, at the American Bounty restaurant, the chef-instructor, Dan Turgeon, put a soup sampler on the menu, one sample of which was turkey consommé. It was so incredibly rich and tasty that Turgeon said, "I will never make chicken consommé again." Ever. Period. I loved how emphatic he was. And there's a great logic to this statement. Turkey is a lot tastier than chicken, and more interesting. And turkey is abundant, available, and inexpensive.

So turkey consommé it is. And here's how it works. The tightly bundled strands of protein in the egg whites unfold in the heat and create a kind of mesh that traps all of the fine fragments responsible for making a clear soup cloudy and dull looking as opposed to bright and clear as tea. It's also an excellent example of crafts-manship in the kitchen, using your knowledge and skill to perfect a common preparation.

This is a fabulous soup to make if you prepare stock from the turkey carcass after Thanksgiving (there's a recipe for turkey stock at ruhlman.com). The key point to remember is that the egg whites also trap some flavor, so it's important to include flavorful ingredients in the egg-white mixture. The soup is fun to eat on its own, but more impressive if you add some garnish so that the clarity shines through.

4 egg whites, lightly whipped

½ Spanish onion, chopped

1 carrot, peeled and chopped

1 celery rib, chopped

12 ounces/340 grams ground turkey

1½ quarts/1.5 liters turkey stock

Optional: chopped plum tomato, fresh thyme, chopped fresh parsley, cracked black pepper-corns, bay leaf

Combine all of the ingredients in a pot, preferably one that is taller than it is wide (too wide a pot spreads out the clarification and allows too much reduction during cooking). Stir the ingredients to distribute the egg white.

Place the pot over high heat and stir vigorously with a whisk. Then switch to a flat-edged wooden spoon, dragging it along the bottom to prevent the egg white from sticking and scorching. As the liquid gets hot, the protein will begin to coagulate and rise to the top. Continue to stir gently to make sure nothing is sticking to the bottom. As the liquid reaches a simmer, the solid ingredients will come together in a mass at the top, known as a raft. As the raft is forming, stop stirring and allow it to come together. Lower the heat before it boils, letting it get hot enough just to simmer over the raft and sink down.

You should be able to see how clear the stock is at this point. Continue to simmer like this for at least 45 minutes and up to an hour. Don't let it boil or the raft will disintegrate. After it's cooked, ladle the consommé through a strainer lined with a coffee filter. Your liquid should be perfectly clear. Taste and add salt if necessary. Serve immediately in warm serving bowls, into which you've divided your garnishes (see below), or cover the consommé and store in the refrigerator until you're ready to reheat and serve.

SUGGESTIONS FOR GARNISH:

2 tablespoons small-diced carrot

2 tablespoons small-diced celery

1 teaspoon vegetable oil

4 shiitake mushrooms, stemmed

1½ tablespoon shallot, finely minced

Blanch the carrot and celery together in boiling water for 20 seconds, then strain under cold running water until thoroughly chilled.

Heat the oil in a small sauté pan over high heat, and sauté the mushrooms for about 1 minute per side. Let them drain on paper towels. Cut them into fine julienne. Combine the mushrooms, shallot, carrot, and celery.

Binder

Orange-Ginger Panna Cotta

SERVES 4

The luxuriously creamy panna cotta (Italian for cooked cream) became a popular dessert in the 1990s when pastry chef Claudia Fleming's buttermilk panna cotta became renowned and much imitated—and for good reason. Like nearly all panna cottas, that one was cream set with gelatin. For a purer flavor, you can instead set the cream with egg whites. It's a great way to make use of extra whites and yields a vegetarian dessert (since most gelatin is made from cow or pig parts). Panna cotta is often served unmolded. But because egg whites are sticky (and don't melt when warmed as gelatin does), serving this panna cotta unmolded is a little trickier, so I recommend serving it in the ramekins in which it was cooked. (If you do want to try to serve it unmolded, use a round ramekin or mold, and oil it first.)

1 cup/240 milliliters heavy cream

½ cup/120 milliliters whole milk

¼ cup/50 grams sugar

Pinch of salt

1 piece of ginger, roughly 2 inches/
5 centimeters long, peeled and thinly sliced

1 whole clove

Peel from ½ orange, pith removed

½ vanilla bean, split lengthwise

4 egg whites

Preheat the oven to 300°F/150°C. Place four 4- to 5-ounce/120- to 150-milliliter ramekins in a large sauté pan or roasting pan and fill the pan so that the water comes three-quarters of the way up the sides of the ramekins. Remove the ramekins and place the pan of water in the oven.

In a small saucepan combine the cream, milk, sugar, salt, ginger, clove, orange peel, and vanilla bean and bring to a soft boil over medium-high heat. Be sure not to burn or scorch the cream, and keep an eye on it as it heats—if it boils over, you'll have a mess and a less tasty panna cotta. Once a boil has been reached, remove the pot from the heat, cover it, and allow it to steep for 1 hour.

In a medium bowl, beat the whites together so they are just combined. Strain the cream base into the egg whites and whisk together. Scrape the seeds from the vanilla bean into the cream mixture. (Put the empty pod in your sugar bowl or bag to gently infuse the sugar.)

Fill the ramekins with the cream mixture. Using sturdy tongs or a spatula or both, place the ramekins in the water bath. Cover the pan with foil—try to do this without moving the pan or the rack, risking water sloshing into the ramekins—and make several slices in the foil to allow the steam to escape. Cook until the panna cotta is set (there should be little to no jiggle when shaken), 35 to 40 minutes.

Remove the ramekins from the water bath, allow to cool, then cover and refrigerate. Serve chilled.

For Body

Clover Club Cocktail

SERVES 4

Without question, one of the finest uses of the egg white is in a cocktail, giving the libation's flavors lovely hang time in the mouth. When we take care to make a great cocktail, we want some lingering, and the body that the protein adds to a cocktail gives the loose fluids this quality. It is also a handy excuse: now you can call your cocktail a protein snack. Many drinks use an egg white—the gin fizz, the whiskey sour, and the following, a cocktail that I learned about via a nifty e-book called Twenty-Five Classic Cocktails. *As with many cocktails, a slight variation changes its name. In this case, if you add ¾ ounce apple brandy it becomes a Pink Lady, also a fabulous drink but not something I'm inclined to order in public. So if this is what you're after, I recommend that you add some Key lime juice instead of the lemon juice and call it a Key Sunrise.*

The white needs to be broken up from its initial viscous state, something bartenders accomplish by giving it a dry shake, that is, a shake without ice; when the egg white has begun to be mixed, ice is added and the drink is shaken further to mix and chill it. I find that it's easier to mix such drinks in a blender, then add the ice, then strain it. This drink calls for grenadine for color and sweetness. It's worth seeking out a true pomegranate syrup rather than a mass-produced grenadine, which is little more than colored sugar water. This cocktail serves four but could easily be doubled in a blender. You could also use a hand blender or a whisk and make a batch in a large glass measuring cup.

6 ounces/180 milliliters gin

2 ounces/60 milliliters fresh lemon juice

2 ounces/60 milliliters simple syrup
(equal parts sugar and water, heated until
the sugar is dissolved)

1 ounce/30 milliliters grenadine
(pomegranate syrup)

2 egg whites

Freeze four martini or coupe glasses.

Combine all of the ingredients in a blender or, if using a hand blender, in an appropriately sized vessel. Blend till frothy. Fill the container with ice and stir for 1 to 2 minutes, then pour through a fine-mesh strainer into the icy glasses.

WHIPPING EGG WHITES

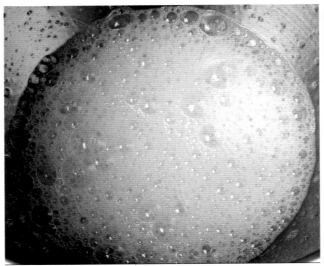

1. / *Egg whites whipped until foamy. This is the stage when you can begin to add the sugar.*

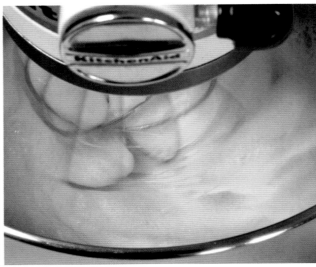

2. / *Whip the egg whites on high, adding the sugar slowly as you do.*

3. / *These egg whites are whipped to stiff, glossy peaks.*

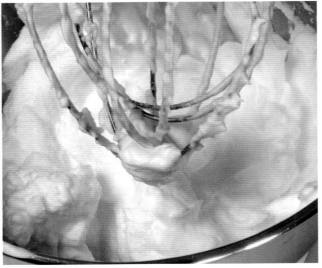

4. / *These egg whites have been overwhipped. Notice the grainy, lumpy texture, compared with the creamy, glossy look of the egg whites in illustration 3.*

The Amazing Meringue

OF ALL THE CULINARY MAGIC MADE POSSIBLE by the egg, perhaps the most extraordinary feats are accomplished when we take the white away from the yolk and whip it into a foam. The white is 90 percent water, but the rest of it is almost entirely composed of protein molecules, tight coils of amino acids. When the proteins are vigorously knocked about with a whisk, they unwind and form webs that capture air bubbles. The egg white's ability to trap infinitesimal bubbles of air, creating what we call a meringue—egg white whipped to many times its initial volume—allows for all kinds of delectable creations in the kitchen.

Meringue leavens cakes, makes chocolate sauce airy for mousse, lightens pastry cream (called Chiboust), and makes soufflés go pouf! Cook a meringue in moist heat, directly in liquid, in a water bath, or in steam, and it becomes a pillowy dessert. Simply bake a common meringue and it becomes a delicious, crunchy confection—a protein-and-sugar cookie—or a shell in which to put other ingredients. Add a little flour and bake the meringue and it becomes angel food cake.

Meringue mixed with hot sugar and honey is the delectable mortar holding together nuts and fruit in a nougat. Mixed with gelatin, meringue becomes marshmallow. Mixed with almond flour it becomes the cookie sandwiching a creamy filling for *macarons*. Mixed with confectioners' sugar it becomes royal icing, a satiny white cream used for decoration. Mixed with sugar and butter it becomes a tasty Italian buttercream icing.

Sugar or some sort of sweetener is always added to meringue for sweet preparations, but how you add the sugar determines the type of meringue you're making. If you simply add the sugar to the meringue while whipping it, it's called a common, or French, meringue. If you cook the egg whites and sugar over a water bath to dissolve the sugar, and then whip it, it's called a Swiss meringue, and if you cook the sugar separately (typically to 250°F/ 120°C or higher) and add it hot to the whipping egg whites, it's an Italian meringue. The amount of sugar varies from chef to chef. A traditional ratio, and what is commonly taught in cooking schools, is two parts sugar to one part egg white by weight. That's a very sweet meringue and about all the sugar the egg-white foam can carry. Many chefs reduce the amount of sugar by as much as half, to as little as equal parts sugar and egg white, which is my preference. Other chefs use confectioners' sugar, which contains some cornstarch and so absorbs water.

Meringues are not stable. They can be over-whipped and become dry and clumpy. If they are left to sit for too long, the water leaks out of them. And they can be difficult to work with if a drop of yolk, or oil, or dish soap somehow gets into your mixing bowl. Acid, in the form of lemon juice or powdered cream of tartar, helps to stabilize egg whites and make a sturdier meringue. As this also balances sweetness, acid is always good to add to meringues. Some chefs, when making a meringue with cooked sugar added late in the mixing, recommend adding a little raw sugar when they start the meringue for stability as well.

Crunchy

Crunchy French Meringue

MAKES ABOUT 32 (2-INCH/5-CENTIMETER) COOKIES

This is the most basic, easiest form of meringue you can make, and it creates delicious cookies. Macarons, shells of meringue mixed with almond flour sandwiching a creamy filling, have all but avalanched this country. It's no wonder, since done well, they're ethereal, and for decades America has known only the coconut ball version. Meringue can also be piped into varying shapes to create a dessert base, such as a shell in which to serve a mousse. My kids simply eat them as they would any crunchy cookie.

A basic ratio for crispy meringue is one and a half parts sugar to one part egg white. An egg white weighs about 1.4 ounces/40 grams, so you would measure by weight 2.1 ounces/60 grams of sugar (seriously, if you're weighing, use your scale's gram button—grams are so much easier to work with). There's plenty of leeway when making meringue—you can reduce the ratio of sugar to egg white to as little as one to one or increase it to as much as two to one.

I always use a standing mixer, but these can be whisked by hand or using a hand blender fitted with the whisk attachment.

3 egg whites

¼ teaspoon cream of tartar
or 1 teaspoon fresh lemon juice

1 teaspoon pure vanilla extract

¾ cup/150 grams sugar

Preheat the oven to 180°F/85°C, or its lowest setting. Line two baking sheets with parchment paper or Silpats and set aside.

Put the egg whites, cream of tartar or lemon juice, and vanilla in a standing mixer fitted with a whisk attachment. Mix on high for 30 seconds, then gradually pour in the sugar. Continue to mix until the meringue is satiny and white and holds gentle peaks.

Pipe or spoon the meringue in whatever shape you wish onto the prepared baking sheets. Put the baking sheets in the oven with the door ajar and bake until the meringues are dry all the way through, 4 to 8 hours (they can't be overbaked if your oven temperature is low; you're really just dehydrating them).

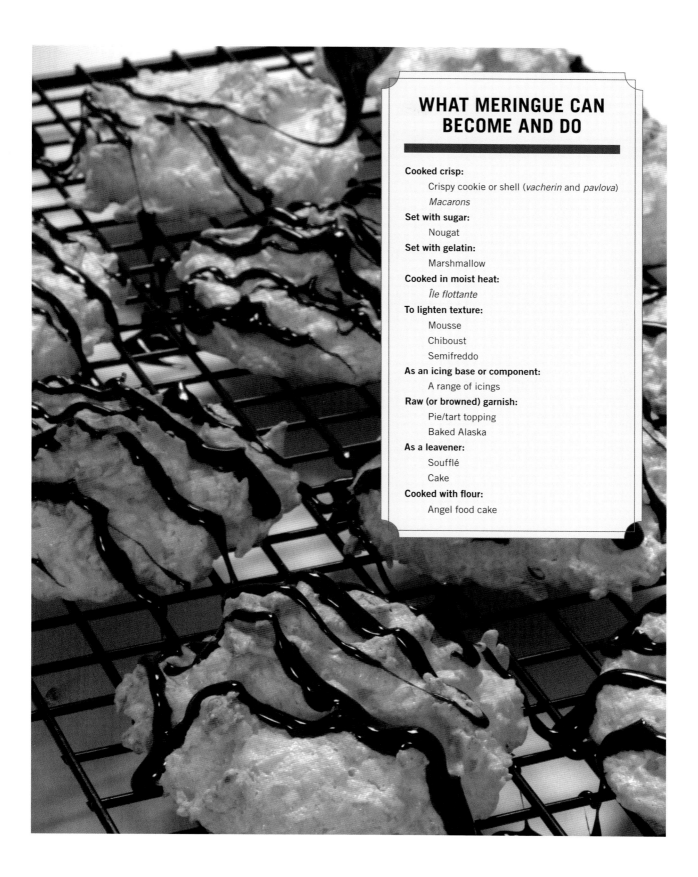

WHAT MERINGUE CAN BECOME AND DO

Cooked crisp:
Crispy cookie or shell (*vacherin* and *pavlova*)
Macarons

Set with sugar:
Nougat

Set with gelatin:
Marshmallow

Cooked in moist heat:
Île flottante

To lighten texture:
Mousse
Chiboust
Semifreddo

As an icing base or component:
A range of icings

Raw (or browned) garnish:
Pie/tart topping
Baked Alaska

As a leavener:
Soufflé
Cake

Cooked with flour:
Angel food cake

Chewy

NOUGAT AND MARSHMALLOWS ARE TWO preparations that are just too cool not to write about. They're similar in construction but very different when finished, largely due to the sugar content and the temperature that sugar reaches. As with most confections, you'll need a candy thermometer to do the job properly. Arguably these are more sugar concoctions than egg preparations, but each relies on meringue to hang the cooked sugar on, as it were. The nougat is hard but chewy, set by the high volume of heavily cooked sugar, and marshmallows are of course soft, meringue set with gelatin.

Nougat

MAKES ABOUT 24 STRIPS

I learned this nougat while working on the Bouchon Bakery *cookbook, wherein executive pastry chef Sebastien Rouxel makes a version for the bakery. I've simplified his recipe for the home kitchen (corn syrup instead of glucose and no cocoa butter, which he uses to get a cleaner cut). But it all basically comes down to the temperature you cook the sugar to; because it's added hot to the egg whites, it ultimately cooks the whites and becomes a foamy white candy into which nuts and fruit are stirred. I love the combination of pistachio, almond, cashew, and cherry, but virtually any toasted nuts or dried fruits can be used.*

3 cups/600 grams plus 1 tablespoon sugar

⅓ cup/100 grams light corn syrup

½ cup/120 milliliters water

1 cup/300 grams high-quality honey, preferably local to you

3 egg whites

Pinch of salt

3 to 4 cups toasted unsalted nuts and dried fruit (a mixture of almonds, cashews, pistachios, hazelnuts, walnuts, dried cherries, cranberries, or anything else you choose)

Combine the 3 cups/600 grams sugar, corn syrup, and water in a high-sided saucepan, bring to a simmer, and cook till it reaches 298°F/148°C, about 10 minutes. Remove the pan from the heat.

In a small saucepan, bring the honey to a simmer and cook it till it reaches 257°F/125°C. Remove the pan from the heat.

Place the egg whites and salt in the clean bowl of a standing mixer fitted with a whisk attachment and beat on high speed. Once a foam has begun to form, add the remaining 1 tablespoon sugar. Continue to beat the eggs until firm, glossy peaks form, 3 to 5 minutes.

Reduce the mixer speed to medium-high and slowly pour in the warm honey. Whip the whites for a few more minutes. Slowly pour in the cooked sugar mixture and continue mixing until the mixture cools to the point that you can hold your hand against the bowl, 15 to 20 minutes.

Replace the whisk attachment with a paddle attachment and paddle in the nuts and fruit.

Line a baking sheet with parchment paper and

1. / *Egg whites heavily whipped with cooked honey and sugar will nearly fill your mixing bowl.*

2. / *Paddle in the nuts and fruit.*

3. / *Spread the nougat out on buttered parchment paper.*

4. / *Cover it with a second piece of buttered parchment and use a rolling pin to flatten the nougat to an even thickness.*

5. / *Slice the uneven edges off to achieve uniform strips.*

6. / *Slice the strips into individual pieces.*

grease it generously with butter. Lay another sheet of parchment on top and rub it well, so that both sheets are equally well buttered, then set aside the top sheet. Butter a rubber spatula or coat it with nonstick baking spray, and scrape the nougat into the center of the buttered parchment on the baking sheet. Cover it with the second buttered sheet of parchment. Use a rolling pin to roll the nougat out to about 1 inch/2.5 centimeters thick. Allow it to cool completely, several hours or overnight, then slice into strips (about 1 by ½ by 6 inches/2.5 by 1 by 15 centimeters). This will keep for a week in an airtight container.

Nougat

Marshmallows

MAKES ABOUT 100 (1-INCH/2.5-CENTIMETER) SQUARE MARSHMALLOWS

For me, marshmallows are an example of how processed food has distanced us from real food. I had a childhood filled with marshmallows out of a bag, whether roasted on a stick over a fire, sandwiched between graham crackers and chocolate, melted and mixed with Rice Krispies, or dropped into steaming mugs of hot chocolate after sledding on dark Cleveland winter afternoons. The realization that one could actually make *marshmallows came only when I was an adult and began exploring and writing about the world of the professional kitchen. As restaurants began to search for more interesting and varied sweet treats and confections, they began offering house-made marshmallows as components of desserts. Marshmallows can be made with gelatin alone or, as here, with a combination of gelatin and egg white. Marshmallows can be flavored with citrus, with jams added to the warm sugar, or, in treating them as a variation on nougat, here with honey. The flavor of the honey is dominant in the finished marshmallow, so use the best-quality honey you can find.*

½ cup/64 grams cornstarch

½ cup/50 grams confectioners' sugar

2 tablespoons unflavored gelatin

¾ cup/180 milliliters water

1 cup/200 grams plus 1 tablespoon granulated sugar

½ cup/170 grams high-quality honey, preferably local to you

2 tablespoons light corn syrup

3 egg whites, at room temperature

¼ teaspoon salt

1 tablespoon pure vanilla extract

Mix the cornstarch and confectioners' sugar together till uniformly combined. Line a rimmed baking sheet with parchment paper and dust it generously with some of the cornstarch mixture.

In a microwavable ramekin, sprinkle the gelatin over ¼ cup/60 milliliters of the water and allow it to absorb the water, or "bloom."

Combine the 1 cup/200 grams granulated sugar, honey, corn syrup, and the remaining ½ cup/120 milliliters water in a medium saucepan over medium-high heat and bring to a simmer. Cook the mixture till it reaches between 265°F/130°C and 285°F/140°C and remove from the heat. Allow the sugar syrup to cool to 210°F/100°C.

While the sugar is cooling, heat the bloomed gelatin in a microwave for 20 or 30 seconds to melt the gelatin.

Place the egg whites and salt in the clean bowl of a standing mixer fitted with a whisk attachment and beat on high speed. Once a foam has begun to form, add the remaining 1 tablespoon sugar. Continue to beat the eggs until firm, glossy peaks form, 3 to 5 minutes.

If the sugar is not cool yet, turn the mixer to low until it is. When the sugar syrup has cooled, turn the mixer to medium and begin to pour the syrup in between the spinning whisk; pour near the side of the bowl.

Once all of the syrup is in the egg whites, add the liquid gelatin and beat on medium-high speed for another 3 to 5 minutes, and then add the vanilla. The marshmallow base will be fluffy and white.

Using a spatula, spread the marshmallow onto the baking sheet with the cornstarch. Spread it toward the corners and continue to spread it out evenly (it should fill about half the baking sheet). Alternatively, you can put the marshmallow base into a piping bag and pipe shapes onto the baking sheet.

Dust the top of the marshmallow with more of the cornstarch mixture and cover it with another layer of parchment. Using a rolling pin or anything with a straight edge, such as a long wooden spoon handle, spread the marshmallow out so that it's smooth and level with the edges of the baking sheet, filling roughly half the sheet. Let the marshmallow set in a cool, dry place for 3 to 5 hours.

Once it is cool and set, cut the marshmallow into squares or other shapes with a pair of scissors or trim with a knife. Keep your scissors or knife clean. Once you cut your shapes, toss them with the remaining cornstarch mixture to coat. They're best eaten that day but can be kept for several days in an airtight container.

Soft

Île Flottante

SERVES 4

I first had île flottante, *floating island, at the French Laundry restaurant in the Napa Valley and fell in love with its texture. Traditionally, meringue is dropped off spoons into sweet simmering milk (filled with air, it floats), cooked for a couple minutes, flipped, and served. The French Laundry bakes tiny ones in small foil cups in a water bath, unmolding for an easy and clean presentation (also filling them with chocolate mousse, serving on a crème anglaise with mint oil, and garnishing with chocolate). I do mine in small ramekins, and I find that steaming them is an easy, fast, and excellent way to cook the meringues.*

Serve with Poire Williams Sabayon made from the yolks and garnish with shaved chocolate or sliced fruit and berries.

4 egg whites

¼ teaspoon cream of tartar or ½ teaspoon fresh lemon juice

1 teaspoon pure vanilla extract

⅔ cup/130 grams sugar

1 recipe Poire Williams Sabayon (page 174)

Butter four 3- to 4-ounce/85- to 115-milliliter ramekins. Place a rack or steamer basket in a pot large enough to hold all four ramekins. Pour in enough water to just reach the rack and bring it to a simmer over high heat.

Combine the egg whites, cream of tartar or lemon juice, and vanilla in the bowl of a standing mixer fitted with a whisk attachment. Begin mixing on high. Slowly pour in the sugar. Continue mixing until you have stiff but still soft, glossy peaks.

Fill each ramekin with the meringue and level off the top. Put them on the rack in the pot of simmering water, cover, and steam until the meringues are puffy and firm, 3 to 4 minutes. These can be unmolded and served warm, left to cool to room temperature, or refrigerated for up to 3 hours and served cold or at room temperature.

To serve with Poire Williams Sabayon, spoon about ¼ cup/60 milliliters of the sauce into the center of each plate and top with an Île Flottante.

Cake

Angel Food Cake with Berry Compote

MAKES 1 CAKE, SERVES 12

Angel food is one of my favorite cakes and it's probably the easiest to be successful with—a meringue into which a little flour has been folded. The flour gives it a bit more structure, a chewiness from the gluten, as compared to a floating island or marshmallow. Like most cakes, this freezes well. It can be made 3 or 4 weeks in advance of using it, if you wish; double-wrap it in plastic and freeze, then let it defrost at room temperature at least an hour before you want to serve it.

I loved angel food cake so much as a boy that my mom created a special version for me that was iced with whipped cream and topped with chopped Heath bars. You can top this cake with some if you like—it will go great with the berry compote as well. It's an easy, lovely dessert for early summertime, when ripe berries are plentiful.

FOR THE CAKE:

12 egg whites

Pinch of salt

1 tablespoon fresh lemon juice

2 cups/400 grams sugar

1 teaspoon pure vanilla extract

½ teaspoon pure almond extract

1 cup/140 grams flour

FOR THE BERRY COMPOTE:

1 cup/140 grams raspberries

1½ cups/210 grams strawberries, sliced

1 cup/140 grams blueberries

½ cup/70 grams blackberries, halved

1 tablespoon fresh lemon juice

⅓ cup/65 grams sugar

Pinch of salt

2 tablespoons Grand Marnier

Preheat the oven to 350°F/180°C.

Whisk the egg whites in a standing mixer with the salt and the lemon juice. Begin to whip at high speed; once the whites are foamy, rain in the sugar, then add the extracts and whip until soft peaks are formed, 5 to 7 minutes in all.

Whisk the flour to break up any clumps. When the egg whites have formed soft peaks, remove the mixing bowl and fold in the flour, one-third at a time.

Scoop the batter into an angel food cake pan or a tube springform pan (a tube pan provides for the biggest rise, but you can use a non-tube pan if you have a way of cooling the cake upside down, which inhibits the cake from sinking as it cools).

Bake until the top of the cake is golden and springs back to the touch, 35 to 40 minutes. Remove the cake from the oven and invert it, still in its pan, on a baking sheet lined with parchment. Allow the cake to cool, upside down, for 1 hour.

While the cake is cooling, make the berry compote. Combine all of the ingredients in a medium saucepan and place over medium heat. Cook until the fruit becomes soft, about 15 minutes. You can use it right away or refrigerate it to serve cool.

Once the cake is cooled, run a knife along the sides to remove the cake from the pan. You may have to give it a good thump to release it from the pan if you are not using a springform pan. Cut into slices and serve with the warm or chilled berry compote.

Part Seven

Egg

Separated but Used Together

Preparations that take advantage of the unique nature of the richness of the yolk by itself and the white by itself are some of the most interesting and dramatic in the kitchen. A cake leavened by egg white is unlike any other kind of cake; a soufflé base, enriched with yolks, leaps out of its ramekin when egg whites are folded into it and baked.

But there are also times when you want to cook the white and the yolk separately and then recombine them as a garnish or as a central preparation. That same soufflé, not baked but rather chilled and eaten, is a mousse. Sometimes their separateness is obscured, the yolk setting the Key lime pie filling, and the white creating the meringue garnish.

But even when separated, they make a dynamic duo.

• • •

Garnish

Leeks Vinaigrette

SERVES 4

In a classic leeks vinaigrette, the leeks are cooked and served in long halves. I'm changing it up here for easier consumption, because even when they're thoroughly cooked they can be tough. And because the egg garnish is so fundamental to the satisfying nature of this dish, slicing the leeks makes the combination of the leek and egg more felicitous and easier to eat. This is a delicious first-course salad that can be made a day ahead, vinaigrette and all, and assembled at the last minute. And it's a great lesson in how a cooked yolk has a smoothing, mellowing, enriching effect on the acidic components of a dish.

8 fat leeks

2 tablespoons/30 grams butter

Salt

⅓ cup/75 milliliters good red wine vinegar

1 tablespoon Dijon mustard

1 raw egg yolk (optional)

Pinch of cayenne pepper

1 cup/240 milliliters vegetable oil

6 hard-cooked eggs, peeled, yolks and whites separated and finely chopped or passed through a sieve or basket strainer

Salt and freshly ground black pepper

Cut the root ends off the leeks, then cut them in half lengthwise. Rinse them thoroughly. Remove the dark green tops and save them for the next time you make stock. Cut each leek half widthwise into ½-inch strips. (If they are still dirty, soak them in cold water to remove the dirt, then strain.)

Melt the butter in a large sauté pan over medium heat, and add the leeks and an aggressive four-finger pinch of salt. Cook gently until tender but not brown, 10 to 15 minutes. When they taste good and are tender, remove them to a plate lined with a paper towel and allow them to cool. Discard any pieces that are brown and papery, as they are likely to be tough.

Make the vinaigrette by combining the vinegar, Dijon, ½ teaspoon salt, raw yolk (if using), and cayenne. Drizzle in the oil, whisking continuously as for a mayonnaise. The yolk will help make it a thick, creamy vinaigrette, which is best for the leeks, but a thin one without the yolk is fine as well. Alternatively, you can use a strong blender with or without the yolk for the vinaigrette, pouring the oil in a thin stream over the other ingredients with the blade running on high until it's too thick to blend; remove the emulsified vinaigrette to a bowl and finish whipping in the oil by hand.

When the leeks are at room temperature, put them in a mixing bowl and add as much of the vinaigrette as suits you; any leftover vinaigrette will keep, covered and refrigerated, for up to 3 days. Either finish the dish now or refrigerate the dressed leeks in a covered container for up to 1 day.

To finish the dish, divide the leeks among four plates, spreading the leeks into a disc shape (use a large ring mold if you have one). Season with salt. Spoon some chopped egg white in a smaller circle on top of the leeks (or fill a ramekin with the egg white and upend it on the leeks), and top with a still smaller circle of chopped yolk (about a tablespoon). Grind pepper over the egg and serve.

Ingredient

Curried Deviled Egg Canapés

MAKES 48 CANAPÉS

These are easy, quick, inexpensive crowd pleasers. The drawback to deviled eggs, though, is that they're too good—you want to eat more than you should. Four halves, with scrumptious yolk and flavorful, spicy mayonnaise in the semi-spherical space left by the yolk, is a meal in itself. So, I've scaled these back to quarter eggs, and in true canapé fashion, I serve them on a crouton to make them easier to eat. Of course you could simply make Curried Egg Salad (page 11)—or any egg salad—and spread it on a crouton for a great canapé, but these look prettier.

If you have a pressure cooker, use it here, as the peeling is guaranteed to be easy (see pages 3–5). Each egg will be sliced lengthwise into quarters; for perfectly smooth and even cuts, a wire cheese cutter is ideal. But if you don't have one, a piece of plain dental floss or thread slips right through a hard-cooked egg. The croutons can be made up to a day ahead and kept in a plastic bag or airtight container at room temperature. The deviled eggs should be made as close to serving time as is convenient; if necessary, they can be made several hours in advance, covered, and refrigerated, but the flavor is best just after mixing.

48 canapé-size bread slices or baguette slices

Salt and freshly ground black pepper

1 dozen eggs, hard-cooked and thoroughly chilled in an ice bath, then peeled

1 recipe curried mayonnaise (page 11)

Cayenne pepper or minced fresh chives, for garnish

Preheat the oven to 300°F/150°C. Toast the bread slices on a baking sheet or rack until crisp, about 10 minutes. Sprinkle them with salt and a grind of pepper.

Quarter each egg lengthwise. Put the egg yolks in a large bowl (for perfectly smooth deviled eggs, pass the yolks through a sieve) and mash them with the curried mayonnaise until the mixture is evenly distributed. Season with salt and pepper to taste.

Place an egg-white quarter on each crouton. Fill a piping bag fitted with a star tip (or a sturdy plastic bag with a ½-inch/12-millimeter hole cut from one corner) with the curried yolk mixture and pipe about a tablespoon onto each egg-white quarter. Garnish with a sprinkling of cayenne or chives and serve immediately.

Mango-Lime Semifreddo

SERVES 12

I love the effect of freezing a meringue, giving what is essentially an ice cream base a lightness it wouldn't otherwise have. I usually see chocolate or mocha or coffee semifreddos, but when my assistant suggested making a citrus semifreddo, it made me think of the orange Creamsicles of my youth, so we went that route. Still it remains a semifreddo: a yolk-sugar base, a flavoring component, whipped cream, and meringue. This fills a big springform pan that serves many, for a good make-ahead warm-weather dessert.

2 ripe mangos

**⅓ cup/75 milliliters fresh lime juice
(from about 3 large limes)**

6 egg yolks

1¼ cups/250 grams sugar

1 tablespoon water

3 egg whites

Pinch of salt

**2 teaspoons grated lime zest
(from about 3 large limes)**

2 cups/480 milliliters heavy cream

Peel and dice the mango and place in a blender. Add the lime juice and buzz until the mango is puréed. Refrigerate it.

In the top of a double boiler (or a metal bowl or saucepan) set over simmering water, combine the egg yolks and ¾ cup/150 grams of the sugar. Whip the eggs and the sugar for several minutes, adding the water midway through, until the mixture is very warm, has quadrupled in volume, and becomes a satiny, ribbony sauce, about 10 minutes in all. Set aside.

In a medium bowl, whip the egg whites with a pinch of salt on high speed. Once foamy, add the remaining ½ cup/100 grams sugar. Whip until firm, moist peaks are reached.

Remove the mango-lime puree from the fridge and begin to fold it into the yolk base. Fold in the lime zest and transfer to a large bowl. Fold the meringue into the puree mixture, one-third at a time, until uniformly combined.

In another large bowl, whip the cream to soft peaks; then fold the cream into the mango-lime base, one-third at a time.

Line the inside of a 12-inch/30.5-centimeter springform pan with plastic wrap. Scoop the semifreddo into the mold, cover with plastic wrap, and place in the freezer overnight. (You can also freeze in individual cups if you prefer.)

Unmold and slice to serve (or serve straight from the freezer if serving in cups).

ON SERVING RAW YOLK

A raw egg yolk is a marvelous thing in and of itself. It can be used as a garnish or as a ready-made sauce of the perfect consistency—rich and luxurious. It can be put on virtually any food and thereby make that food better. Make a dimple in a hamburger and put a yolk there. Top a lemony salad with it. Drop it into a soup. Make it the bull's eye in a potato pancake. It seems to me that the only time it doesn't make the food better is when it's already part of the food. It would be a little ridiculous to put an egg yolk on a custard, or ice cream, or mayonnaise, for example. But simply recognizing that an egg yolk on just about any food makes that food tastier, more visually appealing, and more nutritious, turns you into a better cook.

If you're serving a whole unbroken yolk, you may want to remove (or hide) the two white chalazae at either pole of the yolk; these protein coils keep the egg suspended in the white. Pinch them off if you wish, for presentation, but be warned that they may break open the yolk.

Some people are concerned about the safety of raw eggs, and there can be an issue of their carrying the bacterium salmonella, which can give you some GI distress; if you're otherwise compromised by age or health issues, it can land you in the hospital. I have never worried about it and have never been ill from salmonella that I know of in a lifetime of eating raw eggs (my mom used to drop one into my Carnation Instant Breakfast in the mid-1970s).

What you need to know about bacteria in food generally is this: if the bacteria exists in or on the food, it multiplies at an astonishing rate at room temperature, a rate that increases even more quickly if you make it warmer, say 100°F/38°C. If you've got three yolks in a pot for a hollandaise sauce with a small amount of the bacteria in it, and you keep it warm for several hours, you've got a small bacteria bomb with which to sicken friends and family. Therefore, when working with eggs, keep them cold, or keep them hot for as long as you wish and serve freely, or keep them at room temperature but not for longer than an hour. Do that and you should never have to be concerned about consuming egg in any of its forms.

One of my favorite dishes to serve is beef tartare with a raw yolk as a central garnish. Because we've so abused our land and our animals, this dish presents a double whammy, bacteria-wise—salmonella and *E. coli.* I thumb my nose at the danger and eat away because I treat the situation with care.

I buy eggs from local farms, beg them from friends who raise chickens (yes, even here in Cleveland Heights—thanks, Amelia!), or buy organic eggs from the grocery store. I grind my own meat after rinsing it and salting it. You can never be 100 percent certain that your eggs are free of bacteria. But as long as you keep them out of danger-zone temperatures for more than an hour, you shouldn't have any problems with local eggs (or even factory-farmed eggs) because you haven't let the bacteria multiply to harmful levels.

Ingredient and Garnish

Steak Tartare with Egg Yolk, Capers, and Red Onion

SERVES 4

When I realized that I had cooked yolk/raw white recipes but no cooked white/raw yolk recipes, I asked Twitter for suggestions. Hilmi Ahmad, @hilmiahmad77, who cooks at the Sparrow Bar + Cookshop in Houston, suggested adding the white to steak tartare, which I think is a splendid idea.

This makes a delicious and easy hors d'oeuvre or canapé presented on a platter, with the red onion, capers, and anchovy on the side so people can pick and choose their own garnish. The recipe that follows serves up to eight as hors d'oeuvres.

But here I'm serving the dish in individual portions as a first course or lunch entrée. I'm going Craig Claiborne 1970s-style, forming patties with the garnish and seasoning mixed in, accompanied by a toasted baguette and arugula salad (just before serving, toss four handfuls of arugula with olive oil, give the greens a squeeze of lemon, several grinds of pepper, and a few pinches of salt).

As for those concerned about bad bugs, bacteria don't exist within the muscle of raw beef, only on its surface. So if I'm planning to serve a large portion of raw beef at room temperature, I run cold tap water over it heavily to wash off any surface bacteria. I then pat it dry, coat it in salt, wrap it, and refrigerate it for 1 to 3 days. The salt should—I repeat, should, as this isn't a guarantee—take care of any remaining harmful bacteria, in effect curing the meat. (Never eat large quantities of any kind of raw meat ground at a grocery store; you can get really sick.) Then I cut and grind; I prefer a coarse grind, but a fine grind is good, too; you can chop the meat in a food processor or mince by hand.

1 pound/450 grams beef eye of round

Kosher salt

¼ cup/25 grams minced red onion

1 tablespoon fresh lemon juice (or more to taste)

1 tablespoon red wine vinegar

4 eggs, separated

2 tablespoons capers, chopped

2 to 4 tablespoons extra-virgin olive oil (or to taste)

1 teaspoon fish sauce or 1 anchovy, mashed

1 tablespoon minced fresh parsley

1 tablespoon minced fresh chives

Freshly ground black pepper

16 baguette slices, toasted

Thoroughly rinse the meat under cold running water, then pat dry. Rain kosher salt over all surfaces so that it's uniformly salted, pressing it into the surface. It should be completely coated in salt. Wrap in plastic and put it in the refrigerator for at least 2 hours or up to 72 hours.

Put the red onion in a small bowl, sprinkle with ½ teaspoon salt, and add the lemon juice and red wine vinegar; set aside to rest for at least 10 minutes.

Remove the meat from the refrigerator. Rinse off the salt and pat the meat dry. Cut the meat into 1-inch/2.5-centimeter dice and grind it through the largest die of your grinder (or chop it in a food processor or by hand). The grinding can be done up to 1 day before serving; store the ground meat in a tightly covered container in the refrigerator.

Bring a medium pot of water to a boil over high heat. Strain the egg whites through a large perforated spoon or mesh strainer to remove the less viscous part of the white, and pour the egg whites into the water. Reduce the heat to low and cook them till they're set, a few minutes. Drain the hot water and run cold water over the egg whites until they're completely chilled. Pat them dry and press them through a sieve, ricer, or basket strainer.

In a large bowl combine the ground beef, egg whites, red onion mixture, capers, olive oil, fish sauce or anchovy, and the herbs. Mix it thoroughly with a wooden spoon until the garnishes are uniformly distributed. Taste a teaspoonful and adjust the seasoning with more oil, salt, or lemon juice or vinegar and plenty of black pepper. The mixture can be covered and refrigerated for an hour or two before serving.

To serve, form into four patties and set them each on a plate; make a yolk-sized divot in each patty. Place a yolk in each divot and grind more pepper onto the yolks. Serve with toasted baguette slices and arugula salad (see headnote).

Ingredient

___

Chocolate Espresso Kahlúa Soufflé

SERVES 8

Soufflés have a reputation for being difficult, but in fact they're easy to make, and you can even mix and freeze them ahead of time. The tricky part is timing, because you've got to eat them straight from the oven. The meringue that's folded into the flavorful yolky base (here a simple chocolate pastry cream) is filled with countless little air bubbles that expand and lift that base right out of the cup—but as soon as they cool, they'll shrink, and your little miracle in a ramekin will fall, humiliated by the lack of attention.

So just pay attention to timing and you can wow your family and friends—I've yet to meet someone unimpressed by a soufflé. This one's flavored with espresso powder and Kahlúa, but you can mix and match as you wish. Use Grand Marnier instead of the Kahlúa, for instance.

There are all manner of soufflé recipes out there, but I favor the streamlined efficiency of this one. It doesn't result in an over-the-top rise but rather a gentle one, so that the finished soufflé is powerfully rich and flavorful.

¾ cup/180 milliliters milk

1 tablespoon espresso powder

1 tablespoon unsweetened cocoa powder

1 teaspoon pure vanilla extract

Pinch of salt

6 eggs, separated

¾ cup/150 grams granulated sugar, plus more for coating the ramekins

2 tablespoons flour mixed with 2 tablespoons Kahlúa

¾ cup/150 grams semisweet chocolate chips

1 teaspoon fresh lemon juice

Confectioners' sugar, for dusting

Preheat the oven to 350°F/180°C.

Coat the insides of eight 4-ounce/120-milliliter ramekins with butter. Toss a little sugar around in the cups to coat the insides; pour out the excess.

Combine the milk, espresso powder, cocoa powder, vanilla, and salt in a small saucepan and bring to a simmer over medium-high heat.

Whisk together the yolks and ¼ cup/50 grams of the granulated sugar in a medium bowl till the mixture is uniform and the flour evenly distributed.

Add about ¼ cup of the simmering milk mixture to the yolks while whisking, then pour the yolk mixture back into the pot and whisk over the heat until just before it reaches a simmer. Add the flour-Kahlúa mixture, and whisk until the sauce thickens just as it returns to a simmer, 30 to 60 seconds. Remove the pan from the heat and add the chocolate, stirring just to cover the chips with the sauce so that they'll melt.

While the sauce sits, whip the whites on high speed in a standing mixer fitted with a whisk attachment. Once they're frothy, add the lemon juice, then drizzle in the remaining ½ cup/100 grams sugar while continuing to whip. Continue whipping the egg whites until they hold peaks.

Transfer the chocolate mixture to a large bowl. Fold in the egg whites, one-third at a time, folding slowly and gently until the whites are incorporated. Spoon the mixture into the prepared ramekins, filling them about three-quarters full.

Bake for 30 minutes. Dust with confectioners' sugar and serve immediately.

Chocolate Mousse

SERVES 6

Raw egg white lightens and sweetens a chocolate ganache for a classic chocolate mousse, an easy, make-ahead dessert that is great for entertaining.

4 ounces/120 grams chocolate
(at least 60% cacao)

1 tablespoon unsalted butter

Salt

2 eggs, separated

1 cup/240 milliliters heavy cream

¼ cup/60 grams sugar

In the top of a double boiler (or a metal bowl or saucepan) set over simmering water, combine the chocolate, butter, and a pinch of salt. When about 70 percent of the chocolate has melted, turn off the heat, stir the mixture, and allow it to cool somewhat, 5 minutes or so. Stir in the yolks.

In a large bowl, begin to whip the heavy cream with a whisk. Once soft peaks are reached, rain in 2 tablespoons/30 grams of the sugar. Keep whipping until firm peaks are reached. Transfer the whipped cream to the refrigerator while you prepare the rest of the chocolate mousse.

Be sure to clean your whisk and bowl thoroughly before starting the meringue. Add the egg whites and a pinch of salt. Begin whipping until foamy. Then rain in the remaining 2 tablespoons/30 grams sugar. Keep whipping the meringue until stiff, moist peaks are formed. Set aside.

By now the chocolate ganache should be completely cooled. Remove the whipped cream from the refrigerator and fold one-third of the cream into the chocolate ganache. Once it is mixed in, fold in another one-third of the cream. Once that is mixed in, fold the entire chocolate-cream mixture into the larger bowl with the rest of the whipped cream. Fold until the cream is uniform in color.

Begin to fold the meringue into the chocolate cream, half at a time. Be sure that the chocolate cream and meringue are well combined.

Fill six serving vessels—coupes, large wine glasses, or regular old bowls or ramekins—with the mousse. Cover with plastic wrap and place in the refrigerator for at least 3 hours and as many as 8 hours to set. Serve chilled.

Ingredient and Garnish

Cooked Eggnog

SERVES 4 OR 5

Cooking eggs to make eggnog results in a truly delicious elixir—in effect it's a thin crème anglaise. It has the added benefit of taking care of bacteria for those who have an uncommon fear of salmonella poisoning or who, for whatever reason, must avoid raw-egg preparations (in which case, sadly, you'll also need to omit the meringue in this recipe). When I wrote about this technique on ruhlman.com, one of the commenters said she was grateful for it as she needed to serve eggnog to a lot of seniors (who can be badly affected by salmonella poisoning) at a nursing home, and this was the perfect solution.

I include the recipe because it is a delicious example of raw egg white manipulated into an ethereal garnish. A perfect holiday treat.

1½ cups/360 milliliters milk

1 cup/240 milliliters cream

1 vanilla bean, split lengthwise

Freshly grated nutmeg

4 egg yolks

¼ cup/50 grams plus 2 tablespoons sugar

2 egg whites

1 cup/240 milliliters rum, brandy, or bourbon

Combine 1 cup/240 milliliters of the milk, the cream, and the vanilla bean in a small saucepan, bring it to a simmer over medium-high heat, and remove it from the heat. Add plenty of nutmeg shavings and let the mixture steep for 10 minutes. With a paring knife, scrape the seeds from the vanilla bean into the milk-cream mixture. (Put the empty pod in your sugar bowl or bag to gently infuse the sugar.)

Put the yolks and ¼ cup/50 grams of the sugar in a medium bowl and whisk to combine. Whisking continuously, add the milk-cream mixture.

Fill a large bowl with half ice and half water, and float a second bowl in the ice bath. Set a fine-mesh strainer in the bowl.

Return the yolk-cream mixture to the saucepan and stir it with a flat-edged spoon or heatproof spatula over medium heat until the mixture thickens, a few minutes. It should coat the back of a spoon (you can take it as high as 165°F/75°C if you want to measure). Pour it through the strainer into the bowl set in ice. Add the remaining ½ cup/120 milliliters milk and stir to combine and fully cool the mixture. Cover and refrigerate the eggnog until ready to serve.

To make the meringue, whip the egg whites till frothy, then add the remaining 2 tablespoons sugar and whip to very soft peaks (do this shortly before serving for the best consistency).

For each serving, combine 4 ounces eggnog with 2 ounces alcohol in a tumbler, then add ice, top with a dollop of meringue, and garnish with gratings of nutmeg.

Key Lime Tart with Almond Crust and Meringue Topping

MAKES 1 (9-INCH) TART

I was planning to do a yolk-based lemon tart but had recently been in Key West, so I decided to do a lime version. I love this preparation because it uses the egg in three different ways. The yolks enrich and help set the custard, while the white both helps bind the crust and is the basis for the meringue garnish. You can use a standard pie plate if you don't have a tart mold.

1¼ cups/175 grams almond flour (almond meal)

¼ cup/35 grams all-purpose flour

5 eggs, separated

½ cup/100 grams plus 3 tablespoons sugar

3 tablespoons butter, melted

1 (14-ounce/396-gram) can sweetened condensed milk

½ cup/120 milliliters fresh Key lime juice (or Nellie & Joe's Famous Key West Lime Juice)

1 tablespoon grated lime zest

Preheat the oven to 350°F/180°C. Position a rack in the center of the oven.

To make the crust, combine the almond flour and all-purpose flour in a medium bowl. In a small bowl, lightly whip 2 of the egg whites with 3 tablespoons of the sugar to dissolve the sugar. Add the egg white mixture and the melted butter to the flour mixture. Stir till it all comes together. Press the mixture into the bottom and up the sides of a 9-inch/23-centimeter tart pan.

Bake the crust till it looks appealingly golden brown, 10 to 12 minutes. Set aside to cool.

For the filling, whisk together all 5 egg yolks, the sweetened condensed milk, lime juice, and lime zest in a medium bowl. Pour the mixture into the cooled tart crust.

Bake until the center is set but still moves a bit when the pan is nudged, 20 to 30 minutes. Remove the tart from the oven and allow it to cool completely.

Before serving, make an Italian meringue with the remaining 3 egg whites (equal parts egg white and sugar by weight, cooking the sugar to 250°F/120°C). Pipe or spread the meringue onto the cooled pie and broil the top to brown it lightly or hit it with a blowtorch for color. Serve.

I. / *Use a large star tip for a decorative meringue topping, moving it up and down to form waves.*

2. / *Take care while the meringue is under the broiler: turn the tart pan a few times to make sure it ends up evenly browned.*

Ingredient and Garnish

Traditional Eggnog

SERVES 2

This is a great last-minute treat for two people. You could make a big batch, but I prefer to make a traditional eggnog spontaneously when, say, Donna and I skipped dessert and want something festive, sweet, and rich. Use organic eggs and you shouldn't need to worry about salmonella, though, as noted before, the elderly or anyone with a compromised immune system should probably try the cooked version above or the aged eggnog that follows.

2 eggs, separated

4 teaspoons sugar

½ cup/120 milliliters half-and-half

½ cup/120 milliliters bourbon, rye, or brandy

Freshly grated nutmeg

Combine the yolks and 2 teaspoons of the sugar in a large glass measuring cup. Whisking, pour in the half-and-half, then the alcohol, and whisk to combine.

In a small bowl, whisk the whites till frothy, then add the remaining 2 teaspoons sugar. Continue whisking till it reaches your desired thickness, loose if you want to incorporate it into the drink, stiffer for a more festive-looking drink.

Pour the eggnog into two tumblers filled with ice, garnish with the egg white, and grate nutmeg over the top to finish. (Alternatively, fold the whites into the eggnog, then pour over ice and garnish with nutmeg.)

1. / *Homemade eggnog takes all of about 2 minutes. Combine half the sugar and the egg yolks (1 per person).*

2. / *Whisk in the half-and-half and the bourbon, rye, or brandy.*

3. / *Begin whipping the egg whites.*

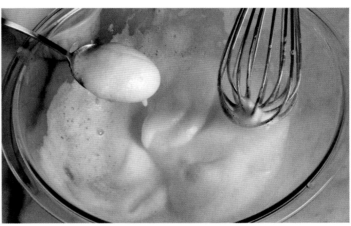

4. / *About midway through, add the remaining sugar. Whip until the egg whites are as frothy as you wish.*

5. / *Pour the half-and-half mixture over ice.*

6. / *Garnish with the meringue and some gratings of nutmeg.*

Traditional Eggnog

Preserved

Aged Eggnog

MAKES ABOUT 3 QUARTS/3 LITERS

Here is a recipe dear to my heart. I first read about it on chow.com and was so intrigued that I tried it myself and wrote about it on ruhlman.com. My friend chef-restaurateur Jonathon Sawyer started making it on a regular basis at his restaurant, trying different combinations of spirits (one favorite is scotch aged in a sherry cask; another uses a coffee-infused rum— you can see the leeway you have here). A little research online revealed that after several weeks the alcohol disables both harmful bacteria and spoilage bacteria, so this recipe will last at least 3 years in the fridge (that's as long as I've managed to keep it without consuming it; you could probably age it for 5 years before it started to taste more funky than is pleasurable—if you try it, email me!). It's well worth making even 3 weeks before serving but takes on a distinctive and pleasing funkiness and color over time.

Serve over ice with grated nutmeg or garnished with a froth of freshly whipped egg whites, as with the Traditional Eggnog (facing page).

12 to 14 egg yolks

1½ cups/300 grams sugar

1 quart/1 liter half-and-half

1 quart/1 liter bourbon

1 cup/240 milliliters Cognac

2 teaspoons pure vanilla extract

Cream the yolks and sugar by whisking them together in a large bowl. Add the remaining ingredients and whisk to dissolve the sugar. Pour the mixture into a plastic or glass container, cover, and refrigerate for at least 3 months.

Serve over ice or straight up with some grated nutmeg and, if you wish, garnished with egg white, whipped to a meringue with sugar.

Acknowledgments

First, thanks go to my wife and collaborator, Donna, whose photography makes these books so valuable to use. Donna employs her camera more as a photojournalist than food photographer. Our goal with photography is to convey information, to show home cooks what they should be able to achieve in their own kitchens. All of the shots in this book were taken in our kitchen or in the makeshift studio we created in our dining room. I am very grateful to those who have written to thank me for the beauty of Donna's photographs, in the books and on the blog, but our main goal is not to induce aesthetic pleasure; rather, we just want to help cooks feel more comfortable in the kitchen. (The aesthetic pleasure is just a happy by-product.) What people don't know is how much Donna pushes me to get things right; where the work is concerned, that is what I thank my partner for most.

I would not be able to get done all that I do were it not for my Michigan-based assistant, Emilia Juocys. In addition to helping create the "Nutritional Differences in Eggs" sidebar in the introduction, she helped develop and test many of the recipes in this book and kept my crazy life somewhat organized. Trained under my colleague on *Charcuterie* and *Salumi,* chef and teacher Brian Polcyn, Emilia has always had my back, and I am grateful to be able to acknowledge her publicly.

This is the fourth book whose recipe selection and testing have been overseen by my Calgary-based colleague, Marlene Newell. In addition to running a fine cooking site called cookskorner.com, a wonderfully warm virtual cooking community, she has tested or overseen the testing of every recipe in this book. If I've gotten anything wrong in a recipe, it's all but certainly my negligence and not hers, as she is tenacious with details. I am also grateful to Matthew Kayahara, an Ontario-based translator

whose love of cooking has led to stages (internships) at many fine restaurants, who was also a lead tester.

I would like to thank the many chefs I've worked with over the years. I've learned from all of you. I'm particularly grateful that, where this book is concerned, I was able to reach out via email to the pastry chefs Michael Laiskonis, Cory Barrett, Shuna Fish Lydon, and David Lebovitz, who helped when sugar and egg whites were making my head ache.

The cake recipes in this book would not have been possible were it not for Donna's sister, Regina Simmons, a professional baker in New York's Hudson Valley, who, as I note in the text, flew in for tutorials on cake basics and decorating (at which I'm particularly lame).

I would like to thank my daughter, Addison, and my son, James, for their forbearance when Donna and I turned the kitchen and dining room, the most trafficked areas of the house, into a photo studio, and for generally putting up with their odd parents, who never seem to leave the house to go to work (quoting one: "Like, what am I supposed to tell my friends you *do?*").

Finally, this book is dedicated to the writer Blake Bailey. I have no friend dearer than he. During the past thirty years, we have shared many apprentice-writer travails, many meals together, and many, many cocktails. I feel it somewhat inadequate, though, as he is a seriously brainy chap who writes massive (and massively praised) biographies of famous writers (John Cheever and Richard Yates, to name two), and here I am dedicating a book on the egg to this august intellect. My ode to the humble egg will have to suffice, Blake. For thee, I conclude with this fine egg anecdote from P. G. Wodehouse, because I know it will please you.

A perilously hungover Bertie Wooster recalls meeting a prospective gentleman's gentleman named Jeeves:

> "If you would drink this, sir," he said, and with a kind of bedside manner rather like the royal doctor shooting the bracer into the sick prince. "It is a little preparation of my own invention. It is the Worcester Sauce that gives it its color. The raw egg makes it nutritious. The red pepper gives it its bite. Gentlemen have told me they have found it extremely invigorating after a late evening."
>
> I would have clutched at anything that looked like a lifeline that morning. I swallowed the stuff. For a moment I felt as if somebody had touched off a bomb inside the old bean and was strolling down my throat with a lighted torch, and then everything seemed suddenly to get right. The sun shone in through the window; the birds twittered in the tree-tops; and, generally speaking, hope dawned once more.
>
> "You're engaged!" I said, as soon as I could say anything.

We may not be able to have our Jeeves, but eggs, and dawning hope, indeed, yes.

Recipe Index by Technique

General Index

Page numbers in *italics* refer to photos.

About the Author

Michael Ruhlman's innovative and successful food reference books include *Ratio, The Elements of Cooking, Ruhlman's Twenty,* and *Charcuterie.* He has appeared as a judge on *Iron Chef America* and as a featured guest on Anthony Bourdain's *No Reservations.* He has also coauthored books with Thomas Keller, Eric Ripert, and Michael Symon. He lives in Cleveland with his wife, photographer Donna Turner Ruhlman, and their two children.

Donna Turner Ruhlman has photographed many of her husband's books, including *Ratio* and *Ruhlman's Twenty,* and is the sole photographer for his blog, ruhlman.com.